Truthformation

John Andrews

ESB Resources
www.esbresources.co.uk

Copyright © John Andrews 2003

The right of John Andrews to be identified as author of this work has been asserted by him in accordance with the Copyright, Designs and Patents Act 1988.

First Published 2003
Second Impression 2004
Third Impression 2007

All rights reserved.
No part of the publication may be reproduced or transmitted in any form or by any means, electronic or mechanical, including photocopy, recording, or any information storage or retrieval system, without permission in writing from the publisher.

Scripture taken from the Holy Bible, New International Version.
Copyright© 1973, 1978, 1984 by International Bible Society.
Anglicisation Copyright © 1979, 1984, 1989.
USed by permission of Hodder and Stoughton Limited.

ISBN 0-9546232-0-7

Published by ESB Resources, Rotherham, England
www.esbresources.co.uk

Design and produced for the publisher by
The North Star Company, Rotherham, England
www.northstarcompany.co.uk

Printed in Great Britain

- Dedication -

To Dawn

My wife, best friend and lover.

Your love for me has never wavered, your belief in me has never weakened and your loyalty to me has never wandered.

My life is complete with you and unimaginable without you.

"Buy the truth and do not sell it;
Get wisdom, discipline and understanding."
Proverbs 23:23

- Acknowledgements -

No project gets to happen without a lot of investment and this has been no exception. Though my name is on the cover as the author, many friends helped to make this dream come true.

My thanks go to:

Dawn, for so much. Her contribution into my life and this project is incalculable. She completes me.

Paul and Rachel Clarkson, who unreservedly believed in my dream to write and wholeheartedly climbed on board, when it was just a tentative whisper. Their support and encouragement has been amazing, and I am thrilled that North Star Company, their own new venture, has produced this book.

The members of Rawmarsh SGN (Small Group Network) in our church. They urged me to just 'go for it', and applauded me when I finished it.

John Bennie, my armour bearer. The servant heart, tireless enthusiasm and deep love he gives me are priceless and humbling. I count him among my dearest friends.

The Senior Leadership of Rotherham New Life Christian Centre, whose generosity enabled me to write this book.

To my Heavenly Father. What a wonderful God You are and what a wonderful life You have given me. I am amazed and grateful.

Thank you one and all!

- Preface -

My 30th year on the planet coincided with my 10th year in full-time Church leadership, a 'job' which I loved then and continue to love with a passion now. However, this period was also a time when I discovered a truly life-changing revelation. I realised that in many key areas I had been ministering the wrong thing, searching for answers when I had been asking the wrong questions. Much of my teaching energy had been devoted to changing 'behaviour', getting people to do the right things and expecting them to follow me simply because 'I was the leader!' It was a deep shock to me to discover that most of this well intentioned and sincere energy had been largely wasted.

It was during a time of personal trauma that I believe God by His Spirit and grace gave me a revelation, which not only changed the way I lived but which transformed my leadership ethos, my ministry value-system and my approach to the Church of Jesus Christ.

What was this revelation?
God impressed upon me this principle, "the key to changing behaviour is through establishing a belief system which is built on a foundation of truth." I became aware that revelation produces our belief system and our belief system produces the power which dictates to our behaviour.

This may be a shock to you as you read, but I had been a Christian since I was eight years old, been through Bible College for three years and been 'leading' a Church for a number of years and I had never made the link between how people behave and what they believe. How had I missed this? However, when 'the penny dropped' and my eyes saw this wondrous truth for the first time, a lot of the stuff I had experienced in those early years of ministry came into focus - good, bad and ugly stuff. If only I had mined this diamond of life much earlier!

Paul urges that instead of being 'molded' to the shape of the planet, we should be completely changed by the 'renewing of our minds' (Romans 12:2). But the only way our minds can be truly renewed is when they have connected with truth. Transformation cannot take place without truth, hence the reason for the title, 'Truthformation'.

This in essence is the subject matter of the book you are about to read. Contained within you will find principles so powerful, that they have radically impacted and revolutionised my life. I commend them to you.

May you know the joy of change through the power of truth.

Dr. John Andrews
Rotherham
2003

- Contents -

1. It Started with a Word..................................9
2. When the Penny Drops............................16
3. Mirror Mirror on the Wall..........................23
4. Faith Creator..30
5. Mind Changer..37
6. Against the Flow......................................45
7. Transformation...51
8. Battleground Truth...................................58
9. Freedom...65
10. The Power of Truth..................................72

Appendix: People of the Word..................79

Also by John Andrews

Rest
Hope
Loved
Mission is like a Box of Chocolates

Moving Beyond Mediocrity
(Published by New Wine Publishing)

Truthformation

It Started with a Word

In 1978, W.P. Kinsella wrote a book entitled *Shoeless Joe*, which over a decade later was turned into the movie *Field of Dreams*. In the opening scene of the film, Ray Kinsella (actor Kevin Costner), is walking through his shoulder high corn field in Iowa, USA, inspecting his crop. In the middle of the field he hears a voice speak to him so clearly that he's certain his wife Annie, sitting on the porch of their farmhouse has also heard it. But no, he's the only one hearing the voice as it speaks the words, 'If you build it, he will come.' The message is repeated a number of times, until Ray works out what he has to build and this in turn sets him on a path to create in his own words, 'something totally illogical.' With the help of Annie, he ploughs up his crop (much to the dismay and amusement of the farming community), and builds a baseball field, and then… sorry, I won't ruin it for you. Get the movie out, it has got feel good written all over it. Watch it with a big bag of Maltesers to hand, oh, and don't forget the tissues. You'll love it. What I can tell you is everyone thought he was crazy, at times he doubted his own sanity. Very few could see what he could see and although he almost went bust and lost his farm, he still believed, because the voice told him to build, so he did. The movie ends with an endless line of cars snaking their way to his insignificant farm and a floodlit baseball diamond, to watch the greatest baseball match in history.

What I love about this movie is that it all started with a whispered word. Ray put his total trust in it and risked everything he had to make it happen. He heard it, believed it, lived it and built it, and all he had was a word from a voice. As he said in the movie, 'until I heard the voice, I'd never done a crazy thing in my whole life.' When *Field of Dreams* was advertised in cinemas the trailer ended with these words, 'sometimes when you believe the impossible, the incredible comes true.

The Bible contains 66 books, 1,189 chapters and millions of words, but it is significant that it all begins with the Voice of God speaking. The journey to *truthformation* starts right at the very beginning. God's first words and actions enshrine principles and patterns for us, which must not be neglected or ignored for from this first glimpse of God and His work we learn an incredible principle of truth;

Everything Started with the Word

In the first 31 verses of the Bible God is heard to be speaking eleven times, usually prefixed by the phrase "And God said..." That's a lot of words, a lot of talk. But who is God speaking to? Why is He speaking at all, why doesn't He just get on with it?

Don't get side-tracked on cosmic conversations. God was revealing to us a principle of life and success that everything of eternal value and power comes out of The Word. Many years later John understood the importance of this, when he began his gospel in a very distinctive way:

"In the beginning was the Word, and the Word was with God, and the Word was God... through Him all things were made: without Him nothing was made that has been made." (John 1:1-3)

John not only clearly identified Jesus as the Word, but crystalises the principle of Genesis chapter one. Everything that came into being that first week did so out of the Word of God. Before every act of God's creative or redemptive power recorded in the Bible – there is a Word.

When God spoke, three wondrous things happened:

The Word revealed the personality of God

Every time God speaks His Word we get an insight, a revelation of what He is like. In fact it is impossible for Him to speak and not reveal something of His nature and character. When God speaks we need to not only understand what He is saying to us, but also what He is saying about Himself.

Was this ever more true than in Jesus? The writer to the Hebrews called Him, "... the exact representation of His (God's) being..." (Heb.1:3) When the Word walked the earth, the personality of God was on plain view to everyone who had the courage to see. When people looked at the Word, they saw what God looked like.

Has God spoken to you? Go back to that word again. Think for a moment, not on what the word said *to you*, but on what the word says *about Him*.

The Word declared the purpose of God

When God speaks, whether it be on the first pages of the Bible, through the mouth of Jesus His Son, or today in the 21st century, it will always reveal something about His purpose. His Word invites us into the process of His purpose so that we may begin to understand not just what He is like, but where He is going and what He wants to do.

When Jesus the Word was on earth He established the Kingdom rule and purpose of God among mankind. His words and actions were driven by purpose. "Come follow Me... the Kingdom of God is within you... blessed are..." Every word Jesus spoke and every action throughout His life was about revealing and declaring the purpose of God.

Another thought about His Word and purpose. He speaks from the end, not the beginning. When we hear the word, we hear it at a certain point on our journey, along our time-line. However when God says it, it is coming out of His completeness, the fact that in His perfect purpose it is already finished.

When God spoke to Moses, the somewhat beleaguered servant asked for a name. He was being asked to return to a world he had run away from a lifetime ago and face the most powerful ruler on the planet. He needed something. God spoke an awesome name, "I AM!" (Exodus 3:14) Moses was hearing the plan for the first time, but God had already seen it through to completion. Moses was moving into the unknown, but God was already there. If Moses understood this, it would transform the way he stood before Pharaoh.

It is an amazing thought that Jesus died on a literal day in history, yet in the economy of God He had already died before the foundations of the earth were laid!

Has God spoken to you? Go back to the word. Remind yourself of what was said. Can you see the purpose of God in these words? Remember I

AM has spoken this... it feels like you are at the beginning, but He is already at the end. Understanding this will help you to approach your purpose with renewed confidence.

The Word released the power of God

A pattern emerges in the first chapter. Every time the Word is released an action of some description takes place. We have seen the principle that 'everything starts with the Word', but now we see the Word producing a pattern. The fact that every time God speaks some form of action takes place, is a pattern that cannot be ignored. When God speaks power is released.

The Word itself has creative power

On at least four occasions the Word God speaks is enough to create or produce. In these instances there seems to be no action from God other than His words.

"And God said, 'Let there be light,' and there was light." (v 3) "And God said, 'Let the water under the sky be gathered to one place, and let dry ground appear.' And it was so." (v 9) See verses 11 and 14 also. When God speaks the record simply adds '*and it was so*'.

The writer to the Hebrews echoes this, "By faith we understand that the universe was formed at God's command..." (Heb.11:3)

There is creative power in the Word itself. The Word, the truth, has so much power that something can be created that was not there before, a way can be made where there was no way and answers can be found to the impossible questions. Sometimes when the Word is released, there is nothing more we can or should do but stand and watch the Word work.

A supreme example of this is given to us in the life of Christ. A message comes to Jesus that a close friend is dying and his only hope demands immediate action. However, Jesus delays and turns up seriously late, by which time His friend Lazarus has been dead four days. Eventually the Master stands before the tomb and does two things. (He had already asked for the stone to be removed from the tomb).

Firstly He prayed. It should be noted that Jesus probably prayed this prayer as much for our benefit as for His. The praying had been done.

Truthformation

This was a glimpse into the intimacy He had with His Father.

Secondly, He spoke. "Lazarus, come out!" (John 11:43) The rest of course is history. Nobody touched Lazarus, no-one was singing, no atmosphere had been created (apart from the smell), Jesus simply spoke and a dead man walked. Right there in Bethany, ordinary folk saw the creative power of the Word at work. Lazarus was now the walking, talking proof.

Check it out. Look at how many times Jesus spoke to sickness or situations and they changed. On many occasions He did not pray for them, He spoke to them!

What has God said to you, to your family, to your church or business? That Word has power. That Word can be creative and can produce more in an instant than we can manufacture in a life-time.

The Word made way for God to work

On a number of occasions God speaks first then follows this with action.

Note the phrases:
> **"So God made..." (v 7)**
> **"God made..." (v 16)**
> **"So God created..." (v 21)**
> **"God made..." (v 25)**

Each of the above actions were preceded by a Word from God. It must be noted that the action was totally in line with the Word spoken. Everything which God does is in line with His declared purpose. He never acts outside of the authority of His own Word.

Jesus, the Word in flesh, or if you like, the Word in action did not come to freelance and live His own way, eventually making it to the cross, rather His life was one of total subservience to the purpose of God, as expressed through His Word. In the last week of His life He made his disciples aware of this powerful truth:

"These words you hear are not My own, they belong to the Father who sent Me." (John 14:24)

"... but the world must learn that I love the Father and that I do exactly what my Father has commanded Me." (John 14:31)

Jesus the incarnate Word submitted Himself to the spoken Word. God's actions are always in line with His Word. This is significant for us because it points to the assuring fact that if God has issued a Word to our lives, or if we have received a revelation of truth from the Bible, then we can expect the actions of God to support the Word and bring it to completion. His actions cannot contradict His Word.

So what has God said to you, directly or through the Bible? If He has spoken then He will invest huge amounts of energy into making it happen. He cannot work against it, He can only work for it!

The Word empowered creation to work

In the creation account God spoke specifically to two areas and in doing so empowered them to be successful. Once the Word was released, power and authority were also granted to ensure the command could actually be fulfilled.

When God made the creatures of the sea and the air He spoke and said: "Be fruitful and increase in number and fill the water in the seas, and let the birds increase on the earth." (v 22) Question: Did it work?

Then again after He had made mankind He said: "Be fruitful and increase in number, fill the earth and subdue it. Rule over the fish of the sea and the birds of the air and over every living creature that moves on the ground." (v 28) Question: Did it work?

The success of these groups was not just due to genetic design but because of the Word spoken by God. God's Word empowered creation to actually do what it had been designed to do. When God speaks there is an empowerment, which comes because of the Word. There is a release of the eternal into the temporal, the infinite into the finite and the divine into the human. In other words, God is not just telling us what to do, but He is giving us the power to do it, power contained in the Word.

There are examples of this in the ministry of Jesus but perhaps none more so than when a fisherman went water walking in Matthew 14:22-36. The disciples were alone, for Jesus had sent them on ahead while He went off to pray. As they struggled with a storm they saw what looked like a ghost coming towards them. After assuring them it was Him, Peter cried out, "Lord if it's You, tell me to come to You on the water." (v 28) To this, Jesus replied with just one word - "Come." (v 29)

Truthformation

What happened next is truly amazing. Peter simply got out of the boat and walked on water. I know... he eventually sank, well almost (for even then, the Word kept his head above water), but the thing is he walked!

But what did he walk on? Yes the water of course, but in truth he was walking on a word, a word uttered by Jesus, a word which empowered a mere mortal to do the impossible. The word issued by Jesus not only revealed the purpose of heaven for that moment, but it contained the power to action what heaven expected in that moment.

Again I ask this simple question, what has God said to you? What has He asked of you? You need to know that the Word not only reveals the purpose of God, but it releases the power of God to help you do what He has asked.

Be encouraged. If He said it, by the power in His Word, **you can do it!**

John Andrews

When the penny drops 2

I managed to get a B in my Maths O level at school, and to this day I'm a bit mystified as to how that happened. Don't get me wrong, I worked hard and revised hard and believe it or not, I actually enjoyed it, but it was never really at the top of my to do list, if you know what a mean. So I'm going to use a word, and for all those who struggled as I did with this wonderful subject, now would be a good time to take a deep breath and think of a beach in the Seychelles. The word is *algebra*. I mean, even the name sounds painful. "I'm sorry sir, you've got algebra... you only have three months to live!!!" To say I struggled with this area of Maths would be like saying Dracula struggles with garlic and a stake... know what I mean? I hated it. Every time we were set a homework for Maths I would pray it wasn't algebra. I would sit in maths and might as well have been in the French class for all that I understood. It really was like a foreign language.

However, there was a day when something strange happened. I was sitting in class and as the teacher wrote equations with A's, B's and X's on the board, I could actually understand it. I remember the excitement of wanting him to ask the question... because I actually knew the answer. Now, I'm not saying I no longer struggled, but I moved to a more confident place, unafraid of algebra anymore, and actually daring it to come up on my O level paper... and yes, it did.

What happened that day? I really don't know. Something clicked in my brain and I saw stuff and knew stuff that up to that moment had all seemed weird and foreign to me. The same thing happened when I learned to drive. I convinced myself that to remember so many things at once was impossible. I knew others were driving, but they were aliens. Yet one day, all that stuff just came together and I was able understand

Truthformation

that which had thus far been outside my grasp. My granny would have said 'Ah, the penny dropped,' an expression which simply means, *you got it*!

Has that ever happened to you? Well if it has, then it is going to make it a whole lot easier for me to explain what revelation is, for revelation is the one major key we need, to move words on a page into truth in our hearts. Without it, it just will not happen.

Let me help you. Look at what Paul says in Ephesians; "I keep asking that the God of our Lord Jesus Christ, the glorious Father, may give you the spirit of wisdom and revelation, so that you may know Him better. I pray also that the eyes of your heart may be enlightened in order that you may know the hope to which He has called you, the riches of His glorious inheritance in the saints, and His incomparably great power for us who believe." (1:17-19a)

Paul makes a clear link for us. Revelation is the key to knowing and knowing is the key to connecting to the purpose of God. It goes back to our initial premise, what we see dictates what we know and what we know dictates how we live. Jesus taught that 'knowing the truth' was the key to living in freedom, but we need to understanding, that revelation is the key to knowing the truth. In fact, we cannot know truth without it. Hence, of all the things that Paul could have continually asked for on behalf of the Church at Ephesus, he asks for the spirit of wisdom and revelation, he asks that their eyes might be opened. Paul knew the power of revelation.

So what is revelation? Defined simply it is 'seeing' something clearly, maybe for the first time, or 'knowing' something truly for yourself. The sight in this context is clear and real, and the knowing of truth is personal and first-hand, not trickle down. In a spiritual sense it's when the penny drops, it's when you truly get it.

I remember going to the optician for an eye test. I had to wear enormous glasses with room to take a dozen or so lens. The first lens left me bewildered. I knew the letters were there... but I could not see them. Then he dropped another lens and that was a little better, then another and another, until eventually he dropped a lens which made the whole thing crystal clear. What had been foggy and out of focus was now as clear as day... I could see clearly for myself.

Revelation is a little like this. The Spirit of God drops a lens into place and suddenly wow, we can see, and what we are seeing was there all along, but now we're seeing it personally and clearly. What a difference a lens makes!

LIFE WITHOUT REVELATION

Okay, let's go on a walk. The walk is found in Luke 24:13-35, and we're joining two chaps who are in desperate need of revelation. Take a moment to read it… it's a great story. This story teaches us the potential danger of a life without revelation and the awesome power that revelation brings, when it is introduced to any scenario.

We're moving in the wrong direction
"Now that same day two of them were going to a village called Emmaus." (v 13)

Undoubtedly they were going there because that is where they lived, but there is more to this journey than just going home, for they were going away from Jerusalem. This journey was taking them away from some crucial things.

They were leaving their friends behind to go home. The same friends they had laughed and cried with, the ones who had stood with Jesus through thick and thin, those who continued to hope and against all odds believe. Their short journey to familiarity was taking them away from the people they needed to be with, their family.

The first sightings had already been reported of which these two people where aware. They even admitted to that (v's22-24), yet they walked home. Their walk was a walk of defeat and disappointment. By going home at such a time they were sending out a clear signal, that they did not believe this and were not hanging around to see what happened.

Living outside a revelation of truth will always take us away from true community and from the place of possibility. We remove ourselves from anything that could remind us of what we thought we knew, or which could possibly provoke us back to faith. We search instead for the comfort blanket of self-pity… and there we hide.

We miss what is right in front of us

Truthformation

"… Jesus himself came up and walked along with them." (v 15)

Now Dr. Luke says that they were actually kept from recognising Jesus (v 16), for there was a purpose in this journey, but it seems incredible that these disciples didn't recognise His voice, the tones, and His style. For whatever reason, they did not see Him and as a result missed something, which was actually right in front of them.

I am always amazed at how two people can sit in a service, apparently hear and feel the same things, and yet walk away with completely different understanding. I remember the story of a lady who was in one of our services the subject of which was the power of God's love. She listened, nodded, smiled and enjoyed, but it hadn't really touched her. Then on the way home in the car, suddenly the penny dropped. She turned to her husband and said, "God really loves me…he loves me!" From that day on she has never looked back. It had been obvious to many, but she had been missing it, now it had become clear, by revelation.

We come to the wrong conclusions
"… we had hoped that he was the one…" (v 21)

Their lack of revelation left them groping in the dark for sense and reason. They were struggling to understand the A's, B's and X's of this particular equation, it just didn't make sense. As a result their conclusions were all wrong and if believed, they would take them even further from security.

Without truth and its revelation to our hearts and minds, we will always in moments of crisis come to the wrong conclusion. I have done it myself and as a leader in ministry I have encountered this from sincere people over and over again.

I remember as a child being taught in Sunday School about Job. I was told he never doubted, never wavered and came out unscathed. But I've read the book of Job and some of his conclusions were well off centre. You don't believe me? Just try chapters 16-17. We are given a glimpse of what can happen to our thought processes when we reason without revelation.

We doubt the believers

"In addition, some of our women amazed us…" (v 22)

Their hearts are revealed in this statement. They recalled the events of the day dispassionately. There is no spark of hope or life about these words… just facts. It is clear they did not believe what they had been told.

When we live outside of revelation truth, not only do we struggle with the truth, but with the truth bringers. We not only react against what people are saying, but against them. We distance ourselves from the company of such people and look down upon them as if we are the ones with truth, not them. Why do you think Thomas was out of the room when Jesus appeared to the ten?

How do you react to others when they speak of their revelation of truth?

These two followers were in a bit of a state. They had hoped, they thought they had believed, they were sure they knew who Jesus was, but now!! What the conversation now revealed was the fact that they were not living on revelation, that they hadn't really heard Jesus, that they didn't really know and that the penny was truly a long way from dropping. However, all that was about to change.

LIFE TRANSFORMING REVELATION

"Then their eyes were opened and they recognised him…" (v 31) The word used for opened here is interesting. It denotes to open thoroughly, like a child seeing for the first time. As Jesus broke the bread the Holy Spirit dropped a lens over their eyes and suddenly they saw for themselves and they saw clearly. Revelation made an immediate impact on them in three dramatic ways;

It made sense of the past
"Were not our hearts burning within us…" (v32)

The immediate past was made clear. As He spoke something was stirring inside them and they knew it was different but they just couldn't put their finger on it. But now it was clear. Now they understood.

But this revelation now made sense of the events not only of the last few days, but of the weeks and months that had led up to it. With this one piece fitting into place, the whole picture was now becoming apparent. I

Truthformation

can almost hear them say, 'why didn't we see this sooner?' The truth is they could not, without revelation first. As the revelation came... it helped them make sense of the past.

It transformed the present
"They got up and returned at once to Jerusalem." (v 33)

How fast do you think you could walk seven miles? I think we could safely say however long it took them to get home, they got back to Jerusalem in half the time. As they went they were probably laughing, crying and discussing, I can almost taste the excitement of that journey, a journey empowered and inspired by revelation.

Nothing has the power to transform today like a revelation of truth. I have experienced days when I was literally a different person by the end than I was at the beginning. Somewhere in that day I had encountered truth, and fresh energy, life and power flowed into my being as a result of it. Instead of dragging my feet I was running, instead of my head being down in despondency, it was now up in faith.

Ever had a day like that? That's what is happening to our two friends. They were not transformed because of something that was going on around them, the transformation took place because of what was going on within them.

It revolutionised the future
"It is true!" (v 34)

What power would this truth give to these men. They had now 'seen' the risen Christ and 'knew' for themselves that this was really true. No one could ever take that revelation away from them, no one could rob them of the day they had supper (almost) with Jesus. They had heard and seen for themselves, it was true!

That's what revelation does. We move from a place of trickle-down spirituality, which seems to work for the pastor and will hopefully work for us, to a place of knowing and seeing for ourselves. We can actually stand up on that issue and say, 'it is true!' This is one of my fears as a leader, that people will do things because I say so, not because they believe so!
Just ask Thomas. He missed Jesus first time round and then after getting back from wherever he was made the infamous boast that unless he could

put his fingers in the nail prints and his fist in the side, he would not believe. No sooner had the words left his mouth, guess who showed up? The Master graciously invited Thomas to do what he had said he would, but Thomas responded as one who has just encountered a revelation, "My Lord and my God." (John 20:28) Tradition tells us Thomas died a martyr's death just outside Madras in India. It's amazing what revelation can do!

The thought crosses my mind, where would these disciples have ended up without revelation? However, those thoughts are a little scary to me. The fact is they saw for themselves and because they saw, they knew and through knowing they lived for Christ and His purposes.

Remember, revelation of truth determines our belief system, or put another way, what we know and what we believe will dictate to the purpose and power of our lifestyle. How you live today is due to what you believe and know, whether that be good, bad or ugly. Don't blame what's around you… try looking within.

Truthformation cannot take place without a revelation of truth.

If revelation be so important, then we need the to penny to drop constantly in our lives.

Therefore:

> Be open to the Holy Spirit every day, invite Him to lead and teach you.
> Be hungry to learn every day, there is always more for us all.
> Be humble to accept every day, even if it at first challenges all you have known.
> Be generous to give every day, to those who will benefit from the power of your revelation.

"Lord Jesus I cannot live right without your truth, so keep my mind open to the possibility of receiving fresh and dynamic revelation today. When it comes, help me to know it, live it and impart it to others." Amen.

Truthformation

Mirror, Mirror on the wall

I'm a member of a local gym not far from my home. My reasons for joining were twofold. Firstly I enjoy physical exercise. No really, I do. As a teenager if I wasn't at church I was either kicking a football, at the Athletics club or playing judo. The second reason was that I believe God has given me a great vision for my life and ministry and I want to devote all of my life to it, so I believe staying healthy is part of the plan. I remember going for my induction, as I walked towards the door I was pumping myself up, hoping not to make a fool of myself in front of all those fitness fanatics. Everything was going fine, so far so good… then I saw them, mirrors, everywhere!! A whole wall of mirrors from floor to ceiling in the area where I would be doing most of my training. In fact my favourite machine the treadmill was positioned facing the mirrors. Wherever I went, I could not escape them… or me! Now for a man who was once described as 'having the perfect face for radio', mirrors can be a challenge, but as I've faced them, quite literally, I discovered an amazing revelation;

Mirrors don't just reflect your image, they reflect your attitude. They not only reflect what you look like, but how you look at yourself. Whether you like them, hate them, ignore them or tolerate them, mirrors have a way of probing for the truth, not just relating to what you look like, but what you actually believe about the person you see. What's your approach to the mirror? See if you can spot yourself.

The Pragmatic Approach

The mirror is simply a tool to help you do what you want to do. You don't focus too much on pruning, just as long as there is nothing hanging out of your nose… that's okay. (Blokes usually identify with this one).

The Deceptive Approach

In this case you see only what you want to see, strategically ignoring the bits you would rather not deal with right now. You might not believe this, but when I was growing up I used to have a favourite mirror. It was in my parent's bedroom and no-matter what was going on, it always made me look better than any other mirror in the house. It might have been the picture of Mel Gibson I'd stuck there.

The Passing Approach

Here you simply glance at the mirror to make sure the main stuff is where it should be. Maybe the last brush of the hair, straightening the tie or checking the teeth. You're there but not for a major overhaul.

The Lavish Approach

Opposite to the above, this is a place of pampering and enjoyment. The longer you stay the better, much to the frustration of those around you… but who cares, your lapping up every minute of it and it's great.

The Apathetic Approach

This is the person who really doesn't care. Now I admire these folks in some ways for their courage and sense of defiance, but over the years I've met a number of people who I wished had cared just a little bit more. This person isn't too bothered by what they see, just as long as they are comfortable. The mirror is there, but it does not dictate to them, regardless of the occasion.

The Honest Approach

In this instance truth rules. You see yourself as you really are, improve where you can, but for the most part, accept who you are, 'warts and all.' (Did I say warts??) I have learned this approach. No matter how much I confess Leonardo Decaprio's looks over my life, it just doesn't happen. So I've decided to improve within all natural means, but out of the joy of knowing I'm okay!

In a strange way, our approach to the Word of God can be very much the same. How we handle it, listen to it, respect it and respond to it, may be captured in some of the above attitudes. Throughout my life, at one time or another, I've probably treated the Word in all of these ways, both benefiting and at times bombing as a result.

Look at what James says; "Anyone who listens to the word but does not

Truthformation

do what it says is like a man who looks at his face in a mirror and, after looking at himself, goes away and immediately forgets what he looks like." (1:23-24)

James is teaching us a powerful principle here. An amazing key in allowing the truth to make the journey into our lives and bring *truthformation*, is by listening to it and then doing what it says. The two things are inexorably linked. They can be separated, but once this takes place, the power of the Word is neutralised in our lives.

I can almost here the echo of the Master's words in the great Sermon on the Mount (Matthew 5-7). Though He uses a different picture, the principle is the same. Jesus describes two builders, one wise and one foolish. The wise man's house stood the test of the storm, while the foolish man's collapsed. Jesus explained in the conclusion of His sermon the reason for this stark difference. The foolish man had only listened, this he likened to sand, whilst the wise man had both listened and obeyed. This was like building on rock.

Jesus didn't want the crowds leaving with great words of oratory ringing in their ears, 'wow, what a sermon.' Rather He wanted people to leave determined not to look lustfully, to go the extra mile, to forgive their persecutors and to live worry free lives. This He knew would be the difference between those riding on the emotional high created by His passion on the sunkissed day, and those who would earnestly go and dig firm foundations of lifestyle obedience to the words they had heard.

HOW'S YOUR HEARING?

On a number of occasions Jesus used the expression when addressing a crowd, "he who has ears to hear, let him hear." Strikingly, when he addresses the churches at Ephesus, Smyrna, Pergamum, Thyatira, Sardis, Philadelphia and Laodicea in the book of Revelation, He uses this expression, because He wants them to get what He is saying. Not just hear it, but listen to it.

My wife has the most incredible ability. She can do multiple tasks and listen to what I'm saying to her without looking at me, all at the same time. I can be talking passionately without taking a breath while she is dealing with something else, totally engrossed it seems and when I try to catch her out by asking, 'what did I just say?' she can often repeat it word for word. Don't you just hate that? Now I'm different. If football is on, Jesus could be in the room talking... and I would miss it. (I can just hear all the women say, 'typical man!')

For me to hear and listen, I have to concentrate. If I'm messing on the computer during a phone call, I miss bits. If I'm watching the news when my children are speaking, they might as well be speaking Chinese. For me to hear well, I must give myself fully to the person who is speaking.

In truth, that is what Jesus is driving at here. He wants us to concentrate on His words, however we do it, but His concern is that we don't just hear it, but that we do it. In fact for Him, the proof of hearing is in the doing.

"Today if you hear his voice do not harden your hearts..." (Psalm 95:8-9)

What can stop us hearing and listening to the Word of God?

Pride

I remember preaching and after the service a visitor came to talk with me. He and his wife had enjoyed the service and he had thought my sermon very 'nice'. (By the way, I hate nice... call my sermons anything, but not nice, got it!) As I listened, the gentleman explained that he hoped my words would touch many in the gathering, but he concluded, 'they don't really apply to me.'

That's the cry of a proud heart. 'You must be talking to someone else mate.' 'Great sermon, I hope they got it.' 'Thank God I'm better than that and I have the humility to accept it.'

When Jesus was explaining to a religious audience that the key to freedom was knowing the truth, they reacted quite aggressively. Their pride came out when they answered, "... (we) have never been slaves to anyone. How can you say that we shall be free?" (John 8:33) Their pride refused to allow them to consider the possibility that they were wrong and the carpenter from 'up north' was right.

What's the answer? A few drops of humility ointment will work wonders. Humility of heart is the fasttest way to improve your hearing. God refuses to engage with a proud or "haughty" spirit, but humility rings His bell, He'll get off His seat for that every time.

Truthformation

Prejudice

When I was in Bible College, having come straight from Northern Ireland, I have to confess that any preaching with an American accent wound me up. Over the years I had subtly developed a prejudice against our transatlantic cousins, the reasons for which are too numerous to discuss. But I had learned to live with it, justify it and use it to my advantage, firing the odd sniper round into my early sermons. It wasn't until I was challenged on my attitude that I realised I had one. Dawn, (soon to be my wife), got right in my face on the issue and told me in no uncertain terms I was wrong and she was right! My prejudice had prevented me from hearing from men and women of God simply because they had the wrong accent. I know it sounds horrible now, but I just went along with it. Thank God for mercy.

We see this again from the opponents of Jesus in the John 8 passage. They reveal their attitude of superiority when announcing, "Abraham is our father…" (v 39) Their whole approach was prejudiced by this assumption and no one was going to tell them otherwise.

I remember debating the case for women in ministry with a 'brother'. He was adamant it wasn't biblical and I attempted to show him one or two possibilities where that theory may not be so airtight. After pointing to wonderful New Testament examples, like Pheobe, Pricilla and Mary I asked him, "so would you concede there is a possibility of women in ministry?" He answered, "no!" "What, not even a little possibility?" He lashed back, "absolutely not!" I realised then, I wasn't dealing with a brother on a journey prepared to hear and debate, I was dealing with prejudice that would never change.

What's the answer? Come to the truth with an open mind. This does not mean to discard all you have learned to this point, but to constantly submit whatever you know to the possibility of greater or even new revelation.

Presumption

'Been there, done that, got the T-shirt.' Presumption takes us to the dangerous place of believing we have gone as far as we can go on any given issue and that there is no reason to explore it further, because we've got it.

Before I entered the ministry I had a 'theological system' of belief. This is not the time to discuss what it was, except to say, that my commitment to that system was at times greater than my commitment to truth. There were times when I tried to make scriptures fit my system, because the power of my presumption was so immense, that I approached the Word convinced the Bible would prove the system, even when friends showed me scriptures which seemed to prove the opposite. I once argued with a friend for hours over the system. Thankfully he's still my friend and we laugh about it now. However, whenever I think of this, I'm embarrassed.

Listen to the presumption in the words of Jesus' audience that day; "We are not illegitimate children... the only Father we have is God himself." (v 41) Now there's the mother, or should I say father of all presumptions. The power of this presumption was such, that it prevented these same people from hearing the words of the Son of God in flesh right before their eyes.

What's the answer? Allow your presumptions to be tested. If they are true then they will stand, but if they are not, then they will fall. Don't spend your life defending your presumptions, but open your life to the promise of truth day by day.

WHAT ARE YOU DOING?

James says; "Do not merely listen to the word, and so deceive yourselves. Do what it says." (1:22)

If we listen and don't act it is like looking at a mirror and immediately forgetting the image. In other words, the look was merely a glance, and the glance was not enough. When we look without remembering it means the look itself made no impression on us whatsoever. It was such a fleeting look that nothing of importance registered. We go to the office and wonder why everyone is looking at us. At last we're being noticed, when really it's the toilet paper stuck on our chin to save us from bleeding to death after shaving. How did we miss it? The look in the mirror was merely a glance.

So it is with the Word, with the Truth. I'm a parent. God has blessed us with three wonderful children. Occasionally they are up to stuff I'm not sure about. So with my best voice of authority I ask, 'What are you doing?' The standard reply is 'Nothing!' When it comes to the Word, this is the wrong answer. If we are truly engaging with the truth, we will

Truthformation

always be doing something. This is how the truth works into our system and brings transformation, because we have the courage and determination to put into action what it actually asks of us, even if that hurts or challenges us. Many miss the power of truth to bring radical transformation because they fail to take the step of doing, relegating the Word to a mere 'snackette' a taster, or in this context a glance.

I taught a series on the power of blessing in our church. As part of that series we talked about the power of the tongue in bringing a curse of destruction on people, or the gift of life in any context. I challenged the congregation on their use of sarcasm as a form of humour. Anything that pulls people down just isn't funny folks, no-matter what alternative comedians say. A young man was listening to that sermon and he decided to take the word of God to heart and change. He had used sarcasm as a weapon many times, but now it would be different. He shared what a struggle it was having to learn a different language, but he persevered and enjoyed the transformation experience.

Why did this happen? He decided to do what he heard. The revelation came to him and challenged him to put this truth into practice. As a result of the Word working, he changed.

The same can happen to you. It isn't easy, no one said it would be, but it is worth it. There is a challenge in looking into the mirror honestly or in digging down to lay a strong foundation. We can always take short cuts, but that will inevitably end in disaster or pain. If you are serious about *truthformation*, then we must be serious about hearing the Word and doing what it says. If we are, we'll change I guarantee it, because the Word guarantees it. Truth is the key to change, but only when we hear and obey. Without these vital ingredients in our lives, we're merely glancing at the mirror and building on sand.

Look and live!

Faith Creator

"You need more faith!" Well tell me something I don't know. That was the challenge put to me by a preacher. In truth, he didn't need to tell me that for I already knew, but the really big question bugging me was, "how do I get more faith?" Do I pray more, read the Bible more, fast more or possibly confess more? I knew what I needed, I just wasn't sure how to get it.

It's funny how challenges force us back to the Word of God to look for answers. This statement concerned me, but in truth what worried me even more was the fact that I did not know how to get more faith, no one had ever taught me that! I went on a search and discovered a life-changing, mind-liberating truth in the Bible. This statement opened my eyes as how faith worked, where it came from, and it showed me the route to getting more.

Listen to Paul; "Consequently, faith comes from hearing the message, and the message is heard through the word of Christ." (Romans 10:17)

Faith comes from hearing the message. If I receive the message or the Word, it has the power to create faith in my life. This set me on a journey of discovering some revelation faith facts that I had previously been unaware of.

FAITH FACTS
Faith cannot exist without the Word

Faith is not an entity in itself, it can only exist through the Word of God. We cannot faith *faith*. To try to do this is to fundamentally misunderstand where faith comes from and how it works. Faith is inexorably linked to

Truthformation

the Word. Without the Word faith dies cut off from its life supply. Faith is created by the Word, sustained by the Word, increased through the Word and is dead without the Word.

If we want more faith, we need to expose our spirits to the Word of God, hearing what God has to say to us through whatever channel He chooses to speak. That is why the hearing process which we've touched on in the previous chapter is so important. If that goes, then our ability to receive faith, to have faith created within us also disappears. Here me now, man and woman of God, no one can simply manufacture faith. The sort of faith which pleases God can only come from the Word of God. You need the Word to have faith.

Hebrews tells us; "… without faith it is impossible to please God…" (11:6) If we come to God we are called to believe that He is, and that He rewards those who seek after Him. But how can we know that He is that He rewards the diligent, unless we've first received some degree of revelation insight into that truth?

The pattern is this. The Word comes first, then faith, then our mighty exploits. When we admire those who do exploits by faith, at the root of it all without exception we will find a Word. Somewhere "God has said," and this has produced the faith and the power to do what seems to be impossible.

Faith is a key to transformation

As has already been established, it is revelation which produces belief system and our belief system which empowers (or otherwise) our lives. Threaded through this whole process is faith. Created by the initial revelation, faith holds together what we believe and produces the energy for amazing life choices and changes.

Hebrews 11 is regarded as a great example of this and a brief look at the work of Word created faith shows us the power it has to transform. Abel's offering was transformed by faith. Enoch's walk was transformed by faith. Noah's purpose was transformed by faith. Abraham's direction was transformed by faith. Jacob's words were transformed by faith. Joseph's future was transformed by faith and Moses' decisions were transformed by faith. Of course I could go on, but I think we get the picture. Faith was a key component in the transformation process for these people. Once created, faith empowered them to move forward into purpose.

Faith for one issue does not mean faith for all issues

This is one of the most amazing and helpful faith facts that I have discovered. I used to believe that faith was faith. That if I had faith, then that was enough for every issue and area of my life. Yet in practice I struggled. I found myself unshakeably believing in the God who could provide for all my material needs, and yet be totally uncertain when I came to pray for the sick. Where was my faith? Well in truth, on the issue of praying for the sick, I didn't have any.

Let me explain. On the issue of my provision, I had received a revelation Word from God that He would take care of me, never leave me and watch over me. I got that Word as a fifteen-year-old before I left home. Wham, a revelation hit my spirit and over my life, although this has been sorely tested, I have always been able to return to that revelation for sustenance and faith. Yet, for years I struggled with the issue of praying for the sick, because at no point had I received a revelation of God as my healer. Don't get me wrong, I've got it theologically, I could write a very good paper on the issue… but as a revelation, definitely not!

The revelation of this truth helped me beyond words. It has liberated me in my own journey to truth and power and it has allowed me to take the burden of guilt off many wonderful Christians, who are struggling with 'lack of faith' in certain areas of their lives, confused because they have faith in other areas.

The truth is, faith for one issue does not necessarily mean faith for another. Abram had faith to leave his home and travel to a land of promise, but it seems he did not have faith to stay in that land during a time of famine? Elijah had faith to take on all the prophets of Baal, but why did he run from Jezebeel?

I love the cry of the honest man in the scriptures who said to Jesus, "Lord I believe, but help me in my unbelief." (Mark 9:24) What was he saying? Jesus I can believe for some stuff, but there are other issues I'm stuck on… can you help me? Of course He can! But we will never get the answers to the faith-less areas of our lives, unless we understand how Word-created faith works in the first place.

Truthformation

The devil knows how faith works

I am going to deal with this fact in more detail in chapter eight, but it is important to know right now that the devil knows the power of Word-created faith, and he knows how it works. That's why he targets us in specific ways.

The enemy never attacks faith – he will always attack the Word! He knows the dynamic link between faith and the Word, he knows that faith cannot live without the Word, therefore he attacks the foundation issue, the life-blood source of faith, the Word. If he can undermine the Word, then he has a route into faith. If he can force a rift between the Word and faith, then he knows faith is dead!

We see this right in the beginning, "Has God said?" The fact that he asks such a question should alert us to the significance of his strategy. He's after the Word. Though he uses many approaches, I believe his design against the Word is three-fold.

Firstly, he wants to prevent the Word from getting to its target. Prevention is better than cure in his book. He knows if the Word and faith conceive together then there is the potential for a powerful kingdom of darkness threatening baby to be born. So, he employs spiritual contraception, by any and every means preventing the conception of the Word. This is seen powerfully in the parable of the sower when the birds come and snatch the seed before it has the chance to do anything. This is by far the most cost effective tactic of the enemy and it works in so many ways.

How often have we gone to church with some issue on our mind that causes us to miss the Word? I would not be surprised, that more Christian families have issues of friction before getting to church than at any other time. You settle down to read the Word and you remember that job that needs doing. You share your thought with someone only to be told that what you've got is garbage. Are you hearing me? His ambition is to cover your heart with a contraceptive, preventing the Word from hitting the target.

Secondly, if he cannot prevent, he will seek to abort. If the Word gets through and creates faith, then his desire is to see that this life ends as soon as possible, before it has the chance to develop, grow and come to birth.

Again we see this in the sower, when the Word grows and is choked out by the thorns. I have to say, this was a shocker to me, that issues as simple as worry could 'choke to death' the Word of life within our hearts.

When Herod got to hear that Jesus was alive and kicking somewhere in his kingdom he set a simple if somewhat crude plan. He would kill all the boys two and under, and in so doing illiminate the competition for the throne. His plan (although he didn't know it) was to extinguish the Word, prevent it/Him from becoming all He was destined to be in the fulness of God's eternal plan.

The Word has come to you and created faith in the area of giving. Watch, a big bill will arrive. Get ready for something to break down in the house that has been working fine for the last 9000 years. Prepare yourself for the testing of the Word. Forget the money issue for a moment, for it isn't about money... it's about truth. The devil is after the Word not your money, for he knows if he gets the Word, everything else is his anyway.

Thirdly, if he cannot prevent or abort, then he will try to corrupt. When the devil quoted Psalm 91 to Jesus during His temptations, it was an attempt to corrupt the written Word. The quote is actually a subtle misquote, putting emphasis on the wrong things, in order to produce a very dangerous and destructive result. (More on that later).

When the serpent spoke to Eve in the garden he words are so revealing; "You will not surely die...for God knows that when you eat of it, your eyes will be opened and you will be like God, knowing good and evil." (Genesis 3:4-5)

Note the corruption:

"You will not surely die." This was a frontal assault on the Word, no holds barred, no pulling of the punches, straight in your face.

"... for God knows..." How does he know what God knows? He is now presuming to speak on God's behalf, understand God's reasoning and know God's mind.

"... your eyes will be opened..." But their eyes were already open. They had been given everything they needed. They had a dynamic relationship with God. How much more did they need to see?

Truthformation

"… you will be like God…" What a cracker! The greatest swindle of all. They were already like God. Adam and Even were more like God than any man or woman born since that day. They were made in the image of God like no others. What a lie and what corruption.

Be careful man and woman of God. The devil knows how Word created faith works and he will attempt to go after the Word in one form or another throughout your life. Guard the Word, remind yourself of what God really said, not what you think He said, and allow nothing or no-one to corrupt it.

Faith is incomplete without deeds

Word created faith is not complete until it finds an outlet in actions, and not just any old actions, but deeds which directly relate to the Word that has been released in your life.

James teaches us that works confirm faith. "… I will show you my faith by what I do." (2:18) A person should be able to discern what we believe by watching how we live. If they looked at our finances they would be able to see what we believe about money. If they looked at our marriage they would be able to see what we believe about our husband/wife. If they looked at our connection to our local church they would be able to see what we believe about God's purpose on the earth.

Over the years I have met so many people with claims to faith. But I have learned to simply watch them for a while and see if what they say matches up to how they live. I remember a man coming to me in my first church, having moved into the area. He liked me, no, more than that, he thought I was the best thing since the Apostle Paul (I must preach that sermon again) and he wanted to get involved immediately! I didn't know the guy from Adam, so I thanked him for his enthusiastic words and then asked him to come and be a part of us for a few months. Get to know us, see who we are and where we're going. Let us get to know you… and then we'll see. Pretty soon he was gone. God had changed His mind on us, and he had changed his mind on me. Funny that. People say a lot of things, but the evidence is shown in the fruit they bear. Our works confirm the absence oo presence of faith.

James also teaches us that works complete faith. "… you see that his faith and his actions were working together, and his faith was made complete by what he did." (2:22)

A cycle is now emerging. The Word creates faith, faith produces works and works complete the work of the Word (and faith) in our lives. We can say we have faith until the cows come mooing home, but until we actually do something, our faith is not complete. Too many of us are waiting for the right moment, for the perfect conditions and then we'll act. I am not encouraging anyone to be presumptuous or reckless, but when the Word creates faith, in order for faith to reach completion, we have to do something about what the Word has said.

Abraham takes Isaac up a mountain to kill him at God's request. He's about to plunge the knife into the son of promise when God steps in, not only with a ram, but with some profound and incredible words. God said; "… now I know…" (Genesis 22:12)

How did God know? Abraham did something. What he did completed the faith which the Word from God had created in the first place. This is the sort of faith that God gets off His seat for. Not stupidity or presumption, not the arrogant rantings of wishful thinkers, but faith created by the Word, which produces actions of power.

On the journey of *truthformation* faith is vital, in fact we cannot make this pilgrimage without it. But it is important we know how it works, so that we can appreciate and embrace Word created faith. This is the faith that pleases God and leads to continual life transformation.

Hear the Word – live by faith.

Truthformation

Mind Changer 5

New years resolutions, ever tried them? Spurred on by the passing of yet another year and inspired by the prospect of beginning a new one with all the hope and promise it holds, many have set themselves new challenges that they are confident will change their lives for the better. Everything from quitting smoking to abandoning chocolate, from not shouting at the kids to being more attentive to our wives or husbands. Gyms undoubtedly soar in membership applications and self-improvement classes are packed out for this is a new day, a new start and a new opportunity to bring real change. 'This is going to be the year I really do it.'

I can remember approaching a New Year with tremendous optimism. I was determined to pray and read my Bible more (not a bad thing of course) and so I set my spiritual 'work-out', that would really produce Mr. Universe spiritual muscles for my life and ministry, or so I thought. By the end of January I had crashed and burned. I had not only fallen behind on the programme, I was off the chart, lost without a trace, in fact, had a rescue party been sent out, they would still be searching for me. The month, which had begun with such positive motivation, ended in dismal failure. Instead of Mr. Universe, I had whimped out, convinced I had failed God and myself, happy to accept holding the door for the doorkeeper in the House of the Lord.

There were two main reasons why I ended up sucking sand that month. The first was purely practical. I set myself an impossible task, I mean Billy Graham would have struggled to keep up with this programme. My enthusiasm had been allowed to recklessly run out of control producing unreachable targets and certain failure. But the second reason was more significant, and one which I didn't understand until some time later. I had not really changed. I was doing good things, not so much for all the wrong reasons, but without the one real reason I needed. I discovered a powerful lesson that in order to change on the outside, something had to change on the inside. The programme was admirable, but it lacked the power of true change on my part and for that reason above all others, it was doomed. Your resolution may have been different from mine, but whether it was chocolate, the gym, diets or prayer, if the mind hasn't been changed on the issue… nothing else will truly change.

Paul said; "Do not conform any longer to the pattern of this world, but be transformed by the renewing of your mind." (Romans 12:2)

The principles Paul gives us are so powerful in this little passage that we are going to spend the next three chapters exploring them. What I discovered here has radically impacted my life, so don't switch off, don't go away, just sit back and fasten your seat-belt.

If we want to live in the reality of *truthformation*, then we must experience mind-change. If you are reading this, having already taken the decision to follow Christ, then you've already experienced what I'm talking about. When you moved from darkness to light, part of that process was not only the redemption of your spirit, but the renewal of your mind. Your mind changed on a number of issues, through that experience. But this is where many Christians leave mind-changing. They believe that what happened at the cross is enough, and that those initial changes are all they need to sustain a life of progress and growth in the Kingdom of God. I hate to burst your bubble, but nothing could be further from the truth. Now hear me carefully, if your only mind-changing experience has been when you met Jesus at the cross, then you are missing the best God has for you. That day you met Christ should have been the beginning of a change process, which should still be kicking in today. If it isn't, then you need to open up your mind to having it changed all over again.

THE TRUTH ABOUT MIND CHANGING
Truth is the life-force of change

For this we need to see the statement Paul made in verse two in its context. In the previous verse Paul urged the believers to "offer" themselves as living sacrifices for one reason, "… in view of God's mercy…"

Throughout the previous chapters, Paul had patiently, methodically and

Truthformation

meticulously outlined dynamic theological principles locked up in God's process of justification by faith. Like a man peeling an onion, he reveals layer after layer of amazing truth that if grasped can change any life. Pointing to this body of truth and the process he has just undertaken he appeals to the believers to offer their bodies and in the context of verse two, their minds, to God – because of truth.

The Bible teaches us clearly that lasting change only comes from Truth. Other change may come from other things, such as guilt, environment, education or indoctrination, but the life-force of change, the power to initiate and sustain change in our lives has to come from truth or else it will run out of steam and fail to produce what it can.

I have the joy, along with my wife Dawn of raising our three children, all of whom are at different stages of development. I've noticed that I can produce change in them by a number of methods. If Simeon does something to his sisters I can demand "say sorry now," and every time, guess what, he does. If I send Elaina to her room, in a few moments she is downstairs apologising for what she has done. If they are threatened with the loss of privileges because of their current behaviour, things quickly change. But this is not real change. Oh yes their actions are real, the expression is real and the response to discipline is very real, but the change expressed does not last. What I've achieved is behavioural modification produced by the conditions of their environment, but what hasn't happened is *truth change*. I once asked my son, "why did you say sorry?" He answered straight back, "because you told me to!" If we want life change in them and in their relationships with each other, then we will have to impress upon them not just what to do, but why they are doing it. When this transition takes place then they will say sorry and behave in certain ways, because they believe that to be the right thing to do, not simply because they were asked to do it.

Church can be like this. Over the years I have met many people who would be comfortable with a leader or pastor telling them what to do, how to think, where to go and what to believe. In fact for some reading this, that's how you were raised. Thinking for yourself was discouraged, everyone was directed to follow the party line. But what happens when the pastor or leader isn't there? What happens when the office is closed and you get the answer machine? What happens when you have to start making life decisions for yourself out of the revelation of truth you have received? Please don't get me wrong, thank God for leaders and pastors who direct us, but when your experience is simply an extension of theirs because you are doing what you are told, not what you believe, then you will struggle to encounter the mind-changing power of truth. You must know the truth in order for it to set you free!!

Surrender comes before renewal

Paul has urged the believers to offer themselves as "living sacrifices" to God, then he moves on to talk of a non-conformist lifestyle, a radical transformation of lifestyle and a renewal of the mind. You cannot hope to experience a radical belief system change, unless you are prepared to first offer your body, your life... all that you are, to God. Many want to 'dabble' with the principles of Christianity to see if they work, and as a result, those same people point to the fact that all they have known is the failure of such principles. However, talk to those who are in it 100% and the story is often very different. For them the principles are not an experiment, they are a lifestyle. They aren't merely dabbling, they are totally committed to doing and as a result are experiencing the power of the truth. If your life is only 50% on the altar, your mind will never be fully renewed. The key to mind-change is the willing and generous offer of our lives to God and the cause of His Kingdom.

Two would-be followers approached Jesus, they were both keen and willing. To the first Jesus said, "Follow me." To this the man replied, "Lord, first let me go and..." The second person pledges his allegiance to Jesus but with a condition, "I will follow you, Lord; but first let me go back and ..." (Luke 9:59-62) Three sobering truths are worthy of note.

Firstly, both called Jesus Lord. They both it seems understood Him as the Boss, as the one to be followed. Neither of them express any theological concern over His quest, it seems they are there with Him. The language is right and everything looks good.

Secondly, both had conditions. I have deliberately not touched on what their excuses were, but the fact remains, although they addressed Jesus as Lord, they were only willing to accept the demands placed on them by His Lordship, when they had first finished whatever it was they needed to do.

Thirdly, Jesus refused to wait for either. The Master explains what needs to be done and then moves on. Though on the surface this seems harsh, Jesus is teaching a powerful truth here. If we come to Him with conditions, no-matter what language we use, He won't wait for us, He'll

Truthformation

just keep moving. That doesn't mean of course that we could not catch up with Him, but it just means, He isn't waiting.

What's the point? If you want the benefits of a changed mind, then you are challenged to throw your lot in with the Kingdom of God, lock, stock and two smokin' barrels. If you don't, then you won't, it's as simple as that.

Number one priority

The renewal of our mind needs to be more than something we will get around to eventually, it must be for those serious about *truthformation*, a number one priority. The key to both living a transformed life and not conforming to the pattern of the planet is in our ability to renew our minds. The idea of the word used here is "to make new", not just to patch up, but to allow new life, new principles and patterns to touch every area of our mind. This is not just moving furniture around the room, but it represents the complete transformation of the room, from stripping and cleaning to replacing the old with the new.

Solomon cautioned us to guard our hearts "above all else" (Proverbs 4:23). For him, the protection and purification of the heart (often used in the Old Testament interchangeably with the mind) was top of the agenda, because when this went, everything else was touched by it. From the heart he warned us, flow all the other issues of life, and they are all impacted by the condition of the heart or mind, for good or ill. These words are echoed by the Master Himself when He cautioned that our words are linked directly to the condition of our hearts (Matthew 12:33-37), and that our actions are controlled and initiated by the principles and patterns which are within us (Matthew 15:1-20). All of us must take the condition of our minds seriously, placing it at the top of our to do list and ensuring that whatever we are fighting for, this remains our chief prize.

In making it your number one priority it will help you to remember the following;

Renewal of our mind is our responsibility

The responsibility of the renewal of my mind, does not belong to my parents, my wife or my friends, it belongs to me. It is easy to find excuses for why we are the way we are, and in my years of ministry, I have heard most of them. Invariably, whatever the excuse, it is usually somebody else's fault. Rarely have I sat in a counselling situation and heard someone say, "yes, it's my fault. I wasn't walking right with God and no-one else can take the wrap for this but me." Usually I hear something like this, "well I did it, but…" It is amazing who gets dragged into the 'but' of excuse making. Leaders are a soft target of course, and "the reason I backslid and slept with the woman is because the pastor just can't preach!"

Sorry, wrong answer. Brave soul still reading this book, you need to hear and hear it good. Your mind belongs to you. You decide what gets in, what goes out, how you think, what you think and how often you think… not me, not your dad, not your pastor… you! The sooner you get a grip of that, the quicker you will move to becoming a mind-changer. The longer you continue to blame everyone else for your condition, the longer you will live without truth and the power to change.

Renewal of our mind is a continual responsibility

When Paul talked of offering our bodies in verse one, the tense he used implied a once for all action. Once offered, it's done. However, as we move into verse two, the tense changes and we have the suggestion from him, that renewal of the mind, non-conformity to the world and transformation of lifestyle are to be continuous actions. In other words, the pilgrimage of *truthformation* doesn't happened in one easy convenient all-inclusive hit (although in Christ we receive all that we need for life and Godliness), but the principles we have received need to be worked out continually in our lives. This is not a sprint, nine seconds and it's over, rather this a marathon, with a lot of running to be done before we hit the tape.

Practical overnight perfection does not happen. That does not mean we use this as an excuse for poor behaviour or we slacken off in our approach to living well. But we do need to place our lives in the context of a journey where day by day, when truth is accepted and applied, our minds change and consequently we change. As a leader it is wonderful to see people change as a result of an encounter with truth based, faith creating, mind changing revelation. The change is real, lasting and inspirational to all around.

No-matter how much you have changed today, your commitment to the process that has brought you so much success and joy today must be as great tomorrow. The process lasts as long as you are alive. This side of

Truthformation

heaven we never reach the place where we have it all, all truth, all change… all done. We must give ourselves to exposing our minds to truth every day of our lives, so that truth can bring the change to our minds, which can in turn empower transformation.

Renewal of our mind is about pattern not just content

As I wind this chapter down, let me challenge you with one final thought. When it comes to the mind, most Christians concern themselves with 'what' they think about, and of course there is tremendous truth in this. Paul gives us clear advice on this when writing in Philippians he states; "… whatever is true, whatever is noble, whatever is right, whatever is pure, whatever is lovely, whatever is admirable – if anything is excellent or praiseworthy – think about such things." (4:8) When it comes to what we should think about, this just about wraps it up. If what you are thinking about doesn't fall into the above category… eject it now. You don't need a list of a hundred 'do not think abouts', you just need to follow the pattern given by Paul and that should sort it.

However, although the Bible is concerned about what we think, it is also vitally concerned with 'how' we think. This is an area where many Christians fail to venture. 'As long as I'm not thinking about pornography… materialism… evil… I'm okay.' Of course it is good you are not thinking about those things, but the Bible wants to take us beyond *what* and into *how*. Throughout the years I have met many good people, raised in church, who 'know' the scriptures, but don't know how to think.

The *how* of how we think is learning to apply the truth to our thought processes. We are challenged to let our thoughts be driven by revealed truth and core values that are kingdom based not planet based. Telling people what they ought and ought not to think about is relatively easy and it's really an issue of control. However, teaching people how to think is much more challenging, but it eventually leads to maturity and freedom.

Paul explains that when our minds are renewed by truth we are able to do something incredible. "Then you will be able to test and approve what God's will is – his good, pleasing and perfect will."

How do you test and approve what God's will is? By learning to think the right way. When our thought processes are governed by anything other than God's truth, His will becomes a fog of mystery to us. We spend unlimited energy trying to work it out and recovering from our own frustration. We can only test and approve His will from a truth renewed mind, for we are doing both the testing and the approving.

As we explore the double-edged impact of lifestyle that in relation to the planet is both non-conformist and in continual transformation, it is vital to remember that both sides are totally dependent on the renewal of the mind.

It's your mind, so mind it well.

Truthformation

Against the Flow
6

Anyone who knows me can tell you of my DIY prowess, not! Sadly when it comes to the 'do it yourself' department of life, I am way down the rankings on the list of achievers. I have friends who it seems can fix anything, turn their hands to most activities and actually hammer nails in straight. Most DIY jobs around our house are handled by Dawn my wife... you want to see her with a power tool. Stand back and marvel. Invariably I do! Recently something (I'm still not sure of the technical term) went wrong in our toilet cistern. We (note the we) didn't have the right part to fix it and the shops were closed, so Dawn improvised and managed to construct a makeshift solution which would have had Bob the Builder glowing with delight. When one of my friends saw it, he was amazed at the genius of it, and as you can imagine, I tried not to take too much of the credit. Seriously, Dawn, you are wonderful, thanks for keeping our house in one piece.

Knowing this, you can imagine the excitement that filled my heart when I actually made something. It was during my secondary school days and because of the split system our school had, those in the grammar stream didn't get to do any hand craft courses. However, on one occasion someone decided it would be a good idea to let the 'brainy' boys in to have a go. Our task was to design and make... wait for it, a butterdish! I can remember the excitement of placing my heated plastic sheet under the press for the moment of truth. As the press went into action, I held my breath, and as I looked, there it was my very own bright red plastic butterdish. With tender care it was packed into my bag and lovingly presented to my mother, whose only response was, 'what is it son?' I wonder if she still has it?

Why am I telling you all this? Well I was reminded of this experience when I stumbled across the word conform. Let me remind you of what Paul said; "Do not conform any longer to the pattern of this world…" The word used here means to *conform in the same pattern, to fashion or shape one thing like another.* Going back to my butterdish, it's the idea of pressing one object (my plastic sheet) into the image, shape or mould of another object (my super mould design). It could literally be said, that the plastic conformed to the mold.

If you are a Star Trek fan, you will be able to identify with this concept immediately when I mention The Borg. The words, 'We are the Borg, resistance is futile,' would strike fear into every enemy. The Borg did not wantonly destroy other civilisations by wiping them out they simply absorbed them into their collective consciousness. Once conformed to the image of the Borg, the person could still in some way be recognised, but everything about them had now changed, their thinking, feeling, actions and aspirations were now bound up in another power completely. They were now pressed into a different mould.

Through the renewing of our minds we are urged to resist conformity to the pattern of the world. The mind renewed by truth is called to become a non-conformist, standing out and going against the flow of the planet type of mind. If our minds are being renewed by truth on a continuous basis we will find it more difficult to conform to the world than to resist it. We disagree with planet Borg. We cannot only resist, but we can make a decisive impact in touching our world and bringing the power of the Kingdom of God to bear on it. Afterall, Jesus did call His followers "the salt of the earth… the light of the world." (Matthew 5:13-14) I love the Sermon on the Mount for it is filled with both religious and social non-conformity. In laying out the principles of the Kingdom, Jesus takes on the mould of the day. He resisted what up to that time seemed to be the irresistible weight of tradition and established another order. "You have heard it said, *but I tell you…*" Jesus in every way went against the flow of His day and urged His would-be followers to do the same.

Some lessons on non-conformity from the great non-conformist of them all.

Going against the flow is a choice

Jesus never forced anyone to do anything. He always gave them a choice. The essence of the spirit of religion is a demand to uniformity and conformity. Religion (whatever the label) does not cope well with mavericks, or individuals who see things differently. However the power of true faith is in its ability to combine the individual into the corporate, without squashing or erasing the uniqueness of the individual. The Bible is at pains to tell us that Jesus had at least twelve disciples, all named and all with different personalities. Not once in the scriptures are they told to be the same as each other. The only conformity Jesus advocated was to do the will and purpose of God. Perhaps if more leaders and churches worked on this rather than on the less important, we would get further. Conformity to the mould of the planet is not a formality, it is a choice. We decide from the platform of a truth renewed mind whether we conform, allowing ourselves to be squeezed into the 'mind-set' of our world or not.

What choices are you making at home, at the office or at play? 'Well everybody cheats, you know what it's like, bitching about the boss is our main past time, what difference can I make anyway?' Are you choosing to conform or go against the flow?

Moses made a choice not to conform. He was born in Egypt, raised in the palaces of Pharaoh and by anybody's standards, had it made. But he made a choice to be different from all that was around him, to live up to whom he believed he actually was and to go against the flow. "By faith Moses... refused to be known as the son of Pharaoh's daughter. He chose to be mistreated along with the people of God rather than to enjoy the pleasures of sin for a short time." (Hebrews 11:24-25)

With a truth renewed mind, you can make choices today regarding your family, faith, finances and future which will set you against the flow of the planet and on track with the Kingdom of God.

Going against the flow is empowered by conviction

Some years ago an initiative was launched against drugs called, 'Just say no!' It sounded great, but it lacked one vital element, conviction! When I was in education I sat in a class filled with fifteen-year-olds. They were watching a video on the dangers of smoking and even though the message being presented was both horrific and tragic, pulling no punches, I looked around the room and observed young people laughing and joking unmoved by anything happening on the screen. Many of them left the school that day and immediately 'lit up'. Unconvinced that they would end up with cancer or collapsing lungs, they continued to do what they had always done. No is a great word – but words just aren't enough to go against the flow and break the moulds that try to press us in. We need convictions which are truth based and Spirit empowered.

Joseph was not only handsome, intelligent, hardworking and trustworthy, he was off limits, and that is a powerful aphrodisiac for some people. Potiphar's wife tried continuously to get him into bed with her, but he just wouldn't give in. His reasons? Maybe he just didn't like sex. Maybe Potiphar's wife was ugly, though somehow I don't think so. The reason he went against the flow in this particular situation is clearly spelt out by him; "How then could I do such a wicked thing and sin against God!" (Genesis 39:1-23)

He said no on the basis of truth, belief and conviction. His convictions were based on his loyalty to Potiphar and his love for God. These two working in tandem, gave Joseph the fortitude to resist where many men would have succumbed. His choice was driven by truth, not hormones.

Going against the flow is expressed through character

Character is the conduit of our belief system. Our behavioural patterns (though affected by other factors) are primarily driven by what we actually believe. If this is true, then character represents the embodiment of what we believe. Our behaviour towards members of the opposite sex, the way we approach our jobs, the things we spend our money on and our response in moments of pressure, will all be revealed through our character.

I know a man who with one lie could have obtained thousands of pounds – but told the truth instead. I know someone who could have walked away from a marriage (and no one would have blamed them) – but they did not. I know someone who could have had a holiday fling – but stayed faithful. I know someone who could have kept their money all to themselves – but decided to share it. Do you know someone like that?

This young man was in the trickiest world of all, politics. With outstanding intellect and ability he rose through the ranks quickly and proved himself over a sustained period of time to be reliable, faithful and trustworthy. But he made enemies along the way who threatened by his influence set a plan to destroy him. Private investigators were hired to dig the dirt. No one gets to be this big without having bent a few rules. The report read; 'With regard to the target, we could find no hint of corruption at any level. His work record is second to none in the whole country. Although not a national, he is loyal and trustworthy, this man Daniel is above reproach.' (Daniel 6:1-5)

Daniel made conviction-based choices not to go with the flow of his world, but to stand up for what he believed and to be different. He was not trying to be awkward or difficult, just true to what he believed God's revealed Word and purpose were for him. He not only resisted the collective consciousness of the political arena, he influenced it for good with righteousness. Many would have concluded resistance was futile, Daniel had other ideas.

Going against the flow is impossible to ignore

The missionary had said to me 'don't worry, the bus will take you into the station, from there it's easy.' Famous last words. I travelled overnight through the Philippines, towards Manila. The plan was to get to the bus station and walk around the corner, catch a taxi and get to the hotel, simple. However the driver had other ideas. For some unknown reason he decided to drop me well away from the station in an area of the city I had no directions for. As I got off the bus at 5 am, I decided to go left, though it was then that I noticed that everyone else was going right. The further I walked the more I felt isolated, not just because of my colour (and the huge suitcase) but because I seemed to be the only person in Manila moving in this direction. I stood out that morning in more ways than one. The story ended happily, I made it, just.

Love it or hate it, when someone goes against the flow you can't help but notice it. Some will dismiss your contra-flow, others will seek to interfere with it, while still others will admire it, and may even decide to do an about turn and go your way.

Jesus said; "You are the light of the world. A city on a hill cannot be hidden. Neither do people light a lamp and put it under a bowl. Instead they put it on its stand, and it gives light to everyone in the house. In the same way, let your light shine before men, that they may see your good deeds and praise your Father in heaven." (Matthew 5:14-16)

Jesus was impossible to ignore. He never went looking for trouble in fact He came only to fulfil the Law. However, everything He believed, represented and practised so flew in the face of that which was around

Him, whether under Rome or the Sanhedrin, it got Him noticed. He healed on the Sabbath, touched lepers and allowed disreputable women to get way too close. He practised without a licence, had a lot of uneducated northerners about Him, frequently taught women and enjoyed eating with tax collectors and publicans. He liked playing with children, dancing at weddings and telling funny stories. He encouraged the payment of taxes to the Romans, the blessing of persecutors and love for neighbours. He said that a Samaritan was good, proclaimed that a Roman Centurion had greater faith than anyone in Israel and hinted that prostitutes would get into heaven before the religious. He attended to the sick, not the healthy and went after the lost, not the found. He was branded, 'a friend of sinners.' All that without writing a book, doing a talk show or getting on to the God-channel. Wow!

As with Jesus, the truth renewed mind empowers us to not only resist the mould of the world and its pattern of thinking and behaviour, but it gives us what we need to actually bring influence and change to the world.

The planet says staying a virgin until marriage is outdated and foolish. They say a man cannot remain faithful to one woman all his life… and why should he? They say debt is a way of life so why worry about it, embrace it. They say that God is dead and the Church is a spent force. Big words indeed and there are a lot of people going in a direction different from the truth renewed mind. So, the question is what are you going to do about it? Are you going to conform, go with it, mix and mingle, or are you going to go against the flow, empowered by Word based convictions, expressed in Godly character and impossible to ignore?

The journey of *truthformation* energises us to resist conformity. With the truth in our minds we not only have the power to withstand being fashioned to the mould and pattern of our planet, but we have all we need to make a different mould, move in a different direction, one, which reflects both the principles and the pattern of the Kingdom.

Resistance is futile? I don't think so!

Transformation

7

I used to love watching a programme called Changing Rooms. For a period British television was obsessed with cooking and home improvement and this was one of the more successful formats, which emerged at that time. The basic concept was to move into a house and change a particular aspect of it, whether it be the living area, kitchen or bedrooms. Although some of the tastes expressed were rather scary (in my opinion) it was amazing to watch the transformation of a room and the techniques used to change it into something completely different. In each case the room fundamentally stayed the same, but the work ensured that the finished product was nothing like the form it had started as.

The format was invariably the same. The room would be stripped completely, leaving nothing but a bare shell, then they would really go to work. Plasterers, painters, decorators, new floors, lights and even furniture would all be installed into the room over a two day period in the hope that it would be exactly what the owner of the house wanted. (Sometimes it was and sometimes… say no more).

When the moment of truth arrived, the owners were brought it with their eyes closed of course and after a countdown, told to open them. The response was either 'wow this is wonderful,' or, well I'll leave that to your imagination. Whatever the style, loved or loathed, the result was always the same, complete transformation!

Let us remind ourselves what Paul said; "… be transformed by the renewing of your mind." The word transformed is spectacular and for those on the journey of *truthformation*, it's a word we need to take to our hearts and cherish. It is made up of two words and the basic meaning we get from them is, 'the change or transfer of form,' from which we get the idea of trans-form. This is not merely tinkering on the fringes this is revolutionary, wholesale change. In fact the word implies a radical change which impacts the internal and the external. The change being referred to here is not just the adaptation of behaviour, like taking off one set of clothes and putting on another. Rather this implies a shift in belief system through a truth-renewed mind, so contributing to a change of form or nature, resulting in a radically different person. This transfer or change of form is something, which happens within and travels without.

An interesting example of this (in the extreme) is the transfiguration of Jesus. The Bible tells us that "… His face shone like the sun and His clothes became as white as light." (Matthew 17:2) What Peter, James and John witnessed happening externally was the result of what was talking place internally. For a moment, these three boys glimpsed the glory of the union of God and humanity, so it no surprise to me that Peter reacted the way he did. Give the guy a break! Years later when describing this event, Peter wrote;
"… but we were eyewitnesses of His majesty." (2 Peter 1:16) They saw the power of transformation demonstrated in a literal physical way. Before their eyes there was a change or transfer of form which impacted on them.

Though less extreme, yet nonetheless just as radical, this is the idea being presented to us by Paul. Through a truth renewed mind, he has instructed us that we can resist the pattern of the planet and not be conformed. He now builds upon this platform by inspiring us with the prospect of radical inner change ,which will impact every area of our lives and the world around us.

One day I am going to write a book entitled, *Things my Granny said which aren't in the Bible*. Over the years I have grown up believing things that were said to me or about me, things which I subtly believed were truth… if not actually in the Bible. As part of the change that has now taken part in my life, I tend to question perceived wisdom, not with arrogance, but against what I now believe the Bible actually says.

Here are some 'change' statements which sound true, but aren't.

Truthformation

Time changes you

If I had a pound (or euro) for every time I heard that, I'd be driving a BMW by now. The other variation to this statement is, time is a great healer. Both are absolutely and totally wrong. Time can neither change nor heal you. What changes you is revelation and truth, and what heals you is mercy and forgiveness.

The only thing time does is put distance between you and an event and add some more years to your life. With the passing of time we may gather a few more grey hairs or loose our hair altogether, see the increase of wrinkles and get out of breath just watching other people exercise… but that's about it. There is a myth that age is associated with wisdom, but over the years I have met people who are thirty, forty years following Christ, with the maturity and wisdom of a child. I've also met sixteen and seventeen year olds, who are getting to grips with God and have wisdom 'beyond their years.' Hear me now, wisdom doesn't come with the passage of time, it comes with the imbibing of truth.

When he started his ministry training his principal instructor gave him the nickname son of thunder. Yet by the end of his life he was known as the apostle of love. Those who have read the New Testament will know him as John, one of the disciples of Jesus. On one occasion as he travelled with Jesus, he got so upset over the opposition they were experiencing that he asked Jesus to call down fire from heaven and burn their opponents up. (I'm sure John was Irish!!) However by the end of his life he wrote these words;
"If anyone says, "I love God," yet hates his brother, he is a liar. For anyone who does not love his brother, whom he has seen, cannot love God, whom he has not seen." (1 John 4:19)

Wow, a bit of a change had taken place in this man's life. What did it? The passage of forty or fifty years? No! In those years he encountered truth, allowing it to impact his mind and bring transformation to his life. If you are waiting for time to change you…you might as well wait for hell to freeze over, it ain't going to happen. Hitting the big 30, 40 or 50 does not guarantee any change in your life, except another birthday. Transformation takes place as we change or transfer form… and that only comes through truth.

If you are waiting for time to heal you… then settle down for a lifetime of pain, because it will take that and more. If you've inflicted pain, show mercy and if you were on the receiving end of pain, forgive. These two agents of truth will bring a change and transfer of form to your life much more effectively than the passage of time!

You can't teach an old dog new tricks

This nonsense is usually used as an excuse not to change because the person has become set in their ways. Well my response to this is threefold:

Firstly, You are not a dog! The last time I looked you were a human being, the pinnacle of God's creation, designed with creativity, unique ability and boundless potential. As much as I enjoy animals and like dogs… they just don't compare to the magnificence of humanity. God is the number one fan of humanity and those who follow Him should be versed in the celebration of all that is good in God's creation.

The Bible says that you and I are "fearfully and wonderfully made," shaped by God's own hands within our mothers womb, known and loved by Him, conceived with purpose and lavished with love. Doesn't sound like a dog's life to me! We can choose to believe we are dogs, and if we do, we'll live like dogs. I tried that, it didn't work for me, and I've found it is much more fun being a Son. As a Son I sit at the table not under it, and as a Son I am called to enjoy life, not endure it. Years ago the Holy Spirit spoke to me in the kitchen of my home; 'Crumbs are for dogs not for children.' That will do for me!

Secondly, how old is old? I love to celebrate the achievements of any of my friends, we do it in our home and in our Church. I was thrilled with a lady called Kath, who at 82 years of age was awarded a certificate for outstanding work on a lap-top computer. Up until being 81, she had never turned a computer on. I am currently learning to play (slowly, very slowly) the piano and I asked my teacher how old his oldest pupil was – he said 64 years old. A couple of years ago we sent out a missions team from our church to Malta, Barbara signed up for that trip. She didn't have a passport, had never been on a plane and had never been out of the country. At 62 years old she became the oldest member at our church to have been one of our teams.

Then there is Tony. As I write this he's approaching the big 70 and yet

Truthformation

he's still eager, strong, passionate for Jesus, full of zeal in service of our Church, a great personal supporter to me and in love with God. After years in church he often comes and tells me how the teaching is helping him, how he's growing and changing, how he is learning new things. How old is old? You decide!

Thirdly, you can learn new tricks, if you want to. Too often our approach to anything is 'I can't,' or 'I've never done this before,' or 'I'm not sure my pace-maker will take the strain.' Sure I understand this, but you can learn new things and do new things, if you really want to. I know each of us have limitations and I'm not denying that, but what I am convinced of is too many of us never get close to the boundaries of our potential

It is amazing what you can do when we allow our minds to be renewed by truth. We can change or transfer form and be empowered to do things that up to that moment we and everyone else around us just did not think was possible.

You can't make a silk purse out of a sow's ear

If you are not familiar with this awful expression, good. But for the purpose of this chapter let me briefly explain. The ethos behind this statement is that some people cannot be made into something better, because of who they are or where they are right now. This is a derogatory statement, designed to humiliate and demoralise. It's filled with fatalism and apathy and no-where can you find anything remotely like it in the Bible. Those who accept this belief system often respond to challenge with the phrase, 'it's just the way I am.'

As a child and young person I used to take things to heart. I'd worry over school work, people's opinions and how I looked. Someone once said of me, 'he's a born worrier,' and it sounded true, so I accepted it. I worried because *that's the way I am*. But then God challenged me on this statement. He showed me I didn't come out of my mother's womb worrying, I came out free, but somewhere along the line, I learned to worry, accepted worry, even embraced worry and so I became a worrier. Today, I hardly worry about anything in fact sometimes I get worried that I'm not worried!

No-matter how you are, I believe in the power of truth to bring transformation. When I look at the Bible, I see a lot of people whom society would have called 'a sow's ear', transformed into someone and something completely different. Let me give you two of my favourite examples.

Shepherd's delight

Samuel was sent to Bethlehem in search of the new king. Jesse obliged by wheeling out all of his sons that he thought were suitable. After seven straight refusals, Jesse looked embarrassed and Samuel looked confused. God had spoken, but where was the king? Samuel asked if there were any more, only to hear this reply: "There is still the youngest… but he is tending the sheep." (1 Samuel 16:11)

Two things worthy of note here. Firstly, he's the boy with no name. It is interesting that Jesse does not use the boy's name rather he's just referred to as "the youngest."

Secondly, he wasn't invited to the show. It seems Jesse is so convinced that David is not good enough for the part that he did not even get an invite to the ceremony. This may have been due to his youth or it may have pointed to the attitude the father had for his son. Either way he wasn't there. However, this youngest, sheep smelling boy was transformed into the greatest King leader Israel ever knew and one of the most outstanding men in the whole of the Bible. It's amazing what truth can do.

What a pain!

The circumstances of his birth (whatever they were) ensured a terrible start for this young man. His mother gave him a name, which beggars belief. She called him Jabez, which means pain. Imagine going to school, sports day and your first day at work with a name like that. Yet this man stands out from the reams of names in the early chapters of Chronicles.

The Bible says: "Jabez was more honourable than his brothers." (1 Chronicles 4:9) But why was he more honourable?

Firstly, he looked up. The record says he cried out to God and looked for God's blessing on his life. Jabez knew by revelation that this was the only way out of his current predicament. The God of heaven was the answer and getting His blessing was the key.

Secondly, he looked out. His prayer was for enlargement. Jabez

Truthformation

understood that the name he was given had the power to keep him small and if he gave into it, he would forever be a small and bitter man. So, instead of spending his life looking inward, feeling sorry for himself and contemplating his navel, he looked out, to enlargement and increase.

Thirdly, he looked forward. He understood more was at stake than just his little life. He realised that his life would affect the lives of those who would follow him. If he remained a pain, 'a sow's ear', then those coming after him would be blighted and hindered by his calamity. For their sake as well as his, he grasped truth, allowing his mind to be renewed thus changing and transferring his form. What a difference the truth makes.

Have you been labelled a sow's ear? Are you the runt, the stupid child who never quite made it? Are you the nameless youngster not invited to the party? Well, if so, you have some decisions to make. You can suck the thumb of self-pity and blame the world, or you can open your mind to truth, allow it to be renewed and empower you to change. Let David and Jabez inspire you to go where you have never gone before.

I have been a Christian almost thirty years and yet I am certain that the last seven or eight years have witnessed some of my most radical change. That does not mean that I did not change before, but now having been prepared to expose my mind to truth and allow the truth to bring renewal, I have known a deep power within to both resist the pattern of the planet and change or transfer form. If I went back to the city of my birth and met old friends who told me, 'you haven't changed a bit,' I would be deeply insulted. The man writing these words is unrecognisable compared to the person who left the shores of Ireland at seventeen. Though years have past, it is truth, which has changed me, and empowered me to do things I never thought possible.

This excites me, not only for myself, but for you too. You can change, you can move to new places and experience new life, by opening up your mind to and embracing God's revealed truth to your life and allowing it to do its work.

> **"Do not conform any longer to the pattern of this world, but be transformed by the renewing of your mind."**

Battleground Truth

It felt like every muscle and sinew in my body was crying out in agony. I had about one minute to go in the final of a Judo competition and believe me, a minute can last a long time. This was my fourth fight of the night. The previous three, which had taken me to the final, I had managed to win without over exerting myself. But the final was very different. Though in the same weight category, the boy I was fighting was bigger and heavier than I was and he was very tough. I had managed to throw him and was in the lead, but that seemed like a million years ago. Since then I was merely holding on. I can still remember people screaming from the side of the mat, my tongue sticking to the top of my mouth, and my knuckles white and stiff and the pain… incredible pain.

When the referee called time, I was so relieved I fell into the arms of my opponent, who graciously did not let me fall. I had won my first Judo gold medal and as I stood on the podium that night pride and joy filled my heart. In front of my home crowd, in the area of Belfast where I had been born and raised, I won, but not without a battle. That event took place when I was fourteen years old and yet I remember it like it was yesterday. The fear, joy, pain and excitement all mixed in to make it a truly memorable night and I learned a powerful lesson; gold comes at a price and you can't get it without paying.

Luke 4:1-13 records one of the greatest fights in all of history. It isn't merely the battle between the devil and the Son of God, or good against evil. This is a battle for truth. The two warriors understand that the gold medal of truth is at stake and if either is not up to the fight, if either whimps out, then the winner will take all and the looser will leave with nothing. Many have missed the principles contained within this

Truthformation

battle in the wilderness because they have simplified it down to a tussle between the devil and the Son of God. If we can see beyond this for a moment and understand that what they are fighting for is more important in this context than who is fighting, then all of us can benefit from the golden nuggets of truth contained within. For although it seems we have the record of two heavyweights slugging it out, this battle for truth is repeated everyday in hotel rooms, kitchens, cars, board rooms and churches the length and breadth of the country. Welcome to battleground truth.

It is naive to think that the devil who knows the power of *truthformation* more than most, will simply leave us alone and hope it all just works out in his favour. The one thing that frightens him the most is a truth-empowered believer. He can cope with most other stuff, but when you and I get it, allow the Word to touch us bringing renewal to our minds, he knows the potential of such power and he will do anything to try and destroy it. His aim (as seen previously, briefly in chapter 4) is to undermine the truth, distract us from the truth, compromise and corrupt the truth and cause a divorce to take place between the truth and our faith. He's good at what he does, but as we see from this passage – he can be beaten.

THE CHALLENGE TO TRUTH

Luke (as with Matthew and Mark) records three temptations specifically that Jesus went through. I am convinced that these were not only literal temptations, but that they also represent other temptations which Jesus may have undergone both in this period and throughout His life. The Bible tells us that He was "… tempted in every way – just as we are…" (Hebrews 4:15) yet He did not fail or give into temptation once.
However, if we probe below each instance of temptation recorded, we see a simple yet powerful pattern of attack emerge from the enemy and one which I believe in one way or another he repeats over and over again.

He attacked the truth about personhood

"If you are the Son of God…" This relates back to what had just happened in the River Jordan, when Jesus was baptised by John. As Jesus came out of the water, God spoke: "You are my Son, whom I love; with You I am well pleased." (Luke 3:22)

The devil was directly attacking the stated Word of God over Jesus' life.

These words were still ringing in His ears when He entered the wilderness. Now the devil was probing to see if Jesus really believed these words and was prepared to hold to them.

One of the truth-zones the devil will seek to probe is our confidence in who we are and whether we believe what God has said about us and to us. If he can undermine or weaken our confidence in our own personhood and what God has said about us, then he has us well and truly on the back foot and even running for the doors.

I remember going to watch Rotherham United play Manchester City in a Division one league match. City had brought thousands of fanatical supporters who more than filled their end of the ground. Rotherham took the lead and the home crowd went wild, but I will never forget what happened next. The entire crowd of the City supporters began to chant and point in our direction. Over and over again they taunted, 'Who are ya? Who are ya?' Looking across at them I can still recall the face of one young skinhead supporter, venomously ranting at the family enclosure where I was. He defiantly asked the question, 'who are ya?' It was quite intimidating.

This is what the enemy does. He defies the Word spoken to us, over us and about us. He ignores our successes and looking into our eyes he venomously rants, 'who are ya?' At this moment, if we are not sure who we are, what God has said to us, we may find our knees will begin to buckle and the desire to run in the opposite direction will rise within us. Sooner or later the devil will challenge this truth-zone and we must be ready with an answer.

He attacked the truth about purpose

"So if you worship me, it will all be yours." (v 7) In essence, although all three temptations are different, they represent exactly the same thing. They are an assault on the purpose to which Jesus had been called, and to which He submitted himself. Again I draw your attention to the baptism. The symbolism of the event must not be lost, for Jesus humbled Himself to the nature and task of a servant, choosing a path that ultimately led to His cruel death. Hence the Father speaks from heaven: "… with you I am well pleased."

If the devil cannot undermine who you are, he will try to stop what you are doing, by hook or crook. He appeals to physical appetites, material

Truthformation

success and spiritual power in an attempt to get Jesus to move off course. But don't be misled, this wasn't about bread or cities or angels, this was about the purity of the purpose of Jesus. If His purpose was corrupted at this stage, the whole shooting match was over.

When I left my first church, I entered a crisis of purpose. My confidence had been severely bashed and I found myself getting the bus every morning to work as a special needs assistant in a large High School. Don't get me wrong, I loved this job and the people I worked with, but I knew this wasn't my calling… this wasn't who I was meant to be. No one was banging down my door for my services and the phone wasn't exactly ringing off the hook, in fact, it wasn't ringing at all. The school where I worked offered me a job in teaching (pending training) and were so impressed with the work I'd done for them, they wanted to keep me. It is hard to describe how that felt, being wanted by somebody… it felt good. I was tempted to take it and Dawn and I wrestled with it for a while, but in my heart I knew it wasn't what God had said. It was good, I'm sure I would have enjoyed it, and positive I would have made a good contribution to many lives, but I could not line it up with what God had said to me or about me.

At such times, tempting times, we have to dig deep, not just into our reserve of strength, but into what we know to be true about why we are on the planet, what God has called us to do and where He has called us to be. Such truth is worth its weight in gold.

He attacked the truth about truth

"For it is written…" (v's 10-11) As alluded to previously, this was a clever and subtle move and one, which could so easily have worked. The devil actually quotes (or misquotes) Psalm 91 and on the surface of it seems to have a case. However a closer looks reveals two powerful omissions;

Firstly, he omitted the context. The whole of the Psalm is soaked in intimacy. It begins, "He who dwells in the shelter of the Most High…" This is our first clue. This Psalm is not about someone acting alone. This Psalm relates to those who have decided to make God their refuge and to align their lives totally with His purpose and plan. The Word must be understood in its setting before it can be applied to any other setting. The devil knew this, but tried it on anyway.

Secondly, he omitted the condition. Heavenly protection is indeed offered, the devil was right, but this was not to be understood in a presumptuous, self-serving way. Again the clue is given for us in the verses just preceding those quoted by the devil: "If you make the Most High your dwelling – even the Lord, who is my refuge, then no harm will befall you, no disaster will come near your tent." (v's 9-10)

It's a small word 'if,' but if Jesus had have thrown Himself off that temple, it would have cost Him and heaven everything. The devil knows the power of the Word and if he can ever so slightly corrupt it, make it say something other than God intended, get us to act on a word that actually isn't there, then he will be laughing all the way to bank. Be careful, hear the word clearly, note what God said to you and don't settle for anything less.

THE CONFIDENCE IN TRUTH

The reaction of Jesus to this onslaught is remarkable and what we learn from this can empower us to take the weapon of truth and use it against our enemy, who seeks only to "steal, kill and destroy."

Jesus responded with the truth

Note three times, "It is written," (v's 4 & 8) and "it says," (v 12). Without getting too technical about every answer, some things I want you to notice. Firstly, each response was Word based. He quotes from the book of Deuteronomy in each instance. This teaches us that the only way to fight an attack on the Word is with the Word. This is the language the devil respects and knows to be true. No other weapons have the effect against a clever and battle-hardened enemy like that of the Word of God used properly. Noise, music, money or power don't scare him at all, in fact he has more of that stuff than we can imagine, but what really scares him is the Word in the hearts and mouths of ordinary believers.

Notice also that Jesus quoted the Word. He didn't have a scroll up his cloak for just such an occasion. He was able to quote it at the proper moment. Ever wondered what Jesus did at the synagogue? Ever wondered how He got such knowledge which amazed the scribes when He was still only twelve? Well the easy answer is that He was the Son of God and knew it all anyway. But what if, He had to learn just like us? What if He had to go and be taught by the Rabbi just like all the other boys? What if He had to memorise parts of the Torah for His bar-

Truthformation

mitzvah? What if, it wasn't just a chore to Him, but a delight? I suggest to you that as He grew, He embraced the Law, learning to know it and love it, so that when such a day of conflict came, He wasn't looking round for the Rabbi, He was able to release the truth that was already within.

I have a theory, I call it the *Sponge Theory*. Basically the idea is this. Whenever we are squeezed whatever is inside us comes out. My granny used to own a mangle. In the days before spin dryers, this contraption allowed someone to squeeze water out of clothes by passing them through two rollers. My granny used it for clothes, but as a child I used it for scientific experiments involving worms and insects. Cruel I know, but the result was always the same... whether clothes or worms, whatever was in, always came out!!!

What comes out when you get squeezed? The Word of God will only come out if it is in there in the first place. Love the Word, read the Word, learn the Word and in moments of conflict, you will hear your mouth say, 'it is written.'

Secondly, each response was to the point. Look at it carefully. Jesus by His response addressed the core principle at the heart of each temptation. If you want to know what each temptation was about, look at how Jesus answers them. Jesus does not get into debate, argument or discussion, He just releases the Word and lets the Word do only what the Word can do.

Many of us fall into the temptation of trying to do the work of the Word. We release the Word, then try to explain it, defend it and direct it. Without sounding over simplistic, we need to learn to just release it and let it do what it will. I admire the Master's resolve not to enter into debate with the devil. He does not afford him any such respect. He releases the Word, like a hunter releases the hounds and lets the Word work.

What a place, to have such confidence in the Word that we speak it and leave it. Enough said, enough done. Sometimes we reason when we need only release. The Word produces rest in Jesus, even though He has been fasting for forty days, is under severe pressure, He's the one at rest, standing firm and secure in the Word of God. He doesn't try to win the argument He just releases and rests in the truth.

Thirdly, each response put Jesus in control. It is interesting to notice that after each reply of Jesus, the devil does not respond with a counter argument. The Word Jesus speaks puts Him in the driving seat, allowing Him to take authority over the situation and give Him the power to conquer.

I hear so many wonderful Christians talk like we are at the mercy of evil, that at any moment the devil can ride in and take everything. But God has not called us to live in holes in the ground, or on the run, He has called us to possess the land, plant and harvest, increase and prosper and live like we are the head, not the tail. The Church is here to reveal the manifold wisdom of God to principalities and powers. We are here to do the wagging, not to be wagged.

If you are tired of being pushed around by the enemy, of feeling like he always has you where he wants you, then get into the Word. Allow the Word to saturate your mind, bringing renewal and empowering transformation and situations where you always seemed to loose will begin to turn. Temptations which always seemed to get you will be conquered and fears that always seemed to dominate you, will be broken. How? Through the power of the truth, through the Word of God. When 'it is written' comes out of your heart – you are in control!

The account tells us: "When the devil had finished all his tempting, he left Him until an opportune time." (v 13)

I suggest to you, that the devil left defeated, not because he was dealing with the Son of God (although I do not in any way minimise this truth), but because the Son of God used the truth. If the devil ran because he was running from deity, what hope have we in the battleground for truth? He ran from Jesus because Jesus knew, lived and released the truth.

Paul called the Word of God the "Sword of the Spirit." This is a weapon of immense power and if used wisely and properly, will bring freedom, joy and victory. Make no mistake the truth which resides in your heart is the number one target of your enemy. If he can get to it, distract you from it, corrupt it or even destroy it, then he has won.

If the truth lives within you, you have all you need to emerge victorious on battleground truth. This is a battle worth fighting and the spoils for us, if we overcome, are out of this world.

Freedom

One of my favourite scenes from the film *Braveheart* occurs towards the end of the movie. William Wallace (Mel Gibson) is facing excruciating torture and death. The crowd is baying for his blood and his torturer is demanding a confession. On and on it goes and even though it's a movie, I'm suffering just watching it. Wallace motions as if he wants to speak, and as the crowd is hushed, he screams at the top of his voice, 'FREEDOM!' Wow, I'm sure that didn't really happen, but the first time I saw this in the cinema, my eyes filled with tears and my goose-pimples had goose-pimples.

As I was writing this chapter, I was disturbed by the screams of my children and their friends. We have a brick shed in our back garden, which the kids use as a den. However, they decided to lock themselves in and even though they had the keys, somehow they could not open it from the inside. So I was summoned from my computer to go on a rescue mission. At first I struggled to get the door open as something had become lodged in the lock, but after a little winkling, I managed to secure the freedom of half a dozen relieved children. I suppose the preciousness of freedom is never fully appreciated until it is threatened or taken away. What a hero! Not quite on a par with William Wallace, but hey, job well done, and I still haven't had my lunch.

Over the last number of years I have become acquainted with many people from all over the world, seeking asylum in Britain. For some the quest is economic freedom, for others it's religious or even political freedom. One man I met just wanted the freedom to change his name. Whatever the reason, the dream is the same and the cost individuals are prepared to pay to try and secure such freedom is deeply challenging. Meeting these 'asylum seekers' and travelling to various parts of the world has helped me appreciate my freedom in a greater way.

Ever visited a prison? Ask any prisoner what they want and freedom will be top of their wish list. Outside of taking a life, depriving someone of their freedom is one of the most powerful and cruel punishments we can inflict. But it isn't just those behind bars that are suffering from lack of liberty. There are people driving Merc's and BMW's just as bound. Children held captive by fear, wives shackled in a loveless marriage, employees fettered in a dead-end job and countless thousands, who have sacrificed the right to live for the reality of mere existence.

Freedom is one of the greatest themes of the human spirit. Name your top five movies and the two dominant themes will either be love or freedom. Authors have made millions on the back of this word, governments have crumbled because young people and children dared to whisper it in secret, and this truth lies at the very heart of God's plan for humankind. This is what Jesus came to establish, the joy of freedom through the rule of the Kingdom of God. As He started His ministry He announced His intent: "... He has sent me to proclaim freedom to the prisoners..." (Luke 4:18) The passion of heaven is people and the ambition of heaven is that all people be free. But how?

"If you hold to My teaching, you are really My disciples. Then you will know the truth, and the truth will set you free." (John 8:31-32)

What will set us free? Knowing the Truth!

We have spent a lot of time on 'knowing' the truth, but I want you to notice again, that knowing is linked directly to the Word of God, bound up in the teachings of Jesus. This isn't about just knowing stuff, or knowing theological facts, this is about knowing the revealed Word of God, taking it to our hearts and allowing it to renew our minds. If this takes place, if we truly know truth, then and only then can we experience the freedom God originally intended humankind to have. The freedom which truth alone can produce can ensure for us a quality of and purpose to life, which money cannot buy, trial cannot steal and disappointment cannot tarnish.

FREEDOM FROM...

In the context of John chapter eight, Jesus is clearly speaking of the freedom from sin. Those caught in sin are 'slaves' to sin, but Jesus came to empower people from the slavery and bondage of sin, to the freedom of truth and faith. Paul carries the theme on when he gloriously concludes: "It is for freedom that Christ has set us free. Stand firm, then, and do not let yourselves be burdened again by a yoke of slavery." (Galatians 5:1)

Both Jesus and Paul taught a very simple yet dynamically powerful principle. Truth empowers us to conquer sin in every area of our lives. Truth enables us to live outside of the grip of sin, so breaking the bias to sin which humankind has been plagued with, instead ensuring a bias to righteousness. In this context Paul informs us that those in Christ, those who know the truth have the power to do a number of things;

Firstly, dead men can't sin. (Romans 6:11) Through the death of Christ, sin and death no longer had mastery over Him and Paul argues, "in the same way", we can count ourselves dead to sin and alive to God. It's hard for a dead man to steal, to lust or covet. Paul is urging us to see the power we have in such a light. This does not mean we are immune to temptation or likely never to sin again, Paul nowhere says such, but rather he is using imagery which allows us to see the potency of the truth that is within us. It is so strong, that we can reckon or count ourselves dead to sin. In other words, we have the power to live beyond the dominance and destruction of sin, which was our former experience.

Secondly, you are the boss. (Romans 6:12) "… do not let sin reign…" Often the excuse is, 'I just can't help it,' 'It just came out,' 'I'm a man, lust is a way of life,' 'it's just the way I am.' I hear all this, but such excuses show an ignorance of the revelation being presented to us by Jesus and Paul. Once the truth comes we are empowered to be the boss, to no longer be the slave to whatever whim takes our fancy. We live in a world, which seems to deny itself nothing. No price is too high and no risk is too great for the need to have whatever we want. It's a world were self-restraint has become a dirty old-fashioned word, yet it is into this world that Paul speaks and tells us – if you have the truth, you are in control.

Thirdly, the choice is yours. (Romans 6:13) "Do not offer the parts of your body to sin…" Here's the deal. The truth has come and is renewing your mind. Suddenly you are confronted with the reality that sin no longer has the power to dominate you, that in fact you are the boss. The power of choice is placed into your hand. You have the power over the TV remote control, the newspapers you read, where your eyes wonder, how you use your credit card and the way you speak. But, how you use truth-produced-freedom, is entirely your choice.

Through this three-fold imagery, the reality of *truthformation* is again presented to us. Paul is not advocating a life of sinless perfection. However, what he is teaching is that sin has no power over us, unless we give it permission. It cannot get in unless we let it in. Now this is not meant to put pressure on us or make us feel condemned, but rather to inspire us to see and live up to the worthiness of such a calling. That sin, that habit, that secret you are carrying can be broken and it can be conquered, if you want to. If you remember who you are and what you've got, the chances are you will make the right choice.

FREEDOM TO...

Jesus did not just call His followers to a life without sin, but I believe He called them to much more. Being a follower of Jesus is not just about 'don'ts', but I believe it is about 'do's!' Looking at Jesus, and going again to see the experience of the first man and woman, we get a glimpse of what freedom we have been called to – the freedom to enjoy.

The pursuit of happiness is enshrined as a right within the American Constitution and I don't think that is a bad thing. However, those serious about *truthformation* come to understand that the pursuit of happiness in itself will not bring full and free satisfaction. When we pursue what is right and true, the result is happiness and we actually enjoy the journey. Afterall, it is with this concept that Jesus started His greatest ever sermon, "Blessed are…"

Through truth God has secured for you the freedom to enjoy life. As a family we once visited Cadbury's World in England. Now if you like chocolate (and if you don't, what's wrong with you?), then this is a must. I have never seen so much chocolate, in fact my kids thought they had died and gone to heaven. Walking into rooms filled with the aroma of chocolate beats Coco Chanel or Calvin Klien any day… wow and double wow! But I have discovered something about chocolate. The enjoyment is not in the digestive process as it mixes with my digestive juices and slides through my intestinal tract. No, the joy is in the eating. Here's a tip when eating chocolate, do it slowly, in fact the slower the better. Now my wife is the world champion at eating chocolate slowly, she makes it last a long time and enjoys every second of it. (Okay, put the book down and go and find some chocolate – enjoy). Feel better? Back to the truth then.

Truthformation

God doesn't just want you to gulp life down and swallow great big lumps of it at once, He wants you to enjoy every mouthful, to savour every moment and as you lick your lips, you are already looking for more. Don't just chew and swallow life, you have God's permission to let it melt in your mouth.

Looking at pre-fall man and woman in a world without sin, their priorities were different.

Freedom to enjoy God

God would come down to the garden in the cool of the day to walk and talk with Adam and Eve. I can just imagine the joy of these moments and the innocence and intimacy that all would experience. There was no other focus, no other ambition, only to love, worship and serve God. Note what happened when sin entered, "… they hid from the Lord…" (Genesis 3:8) When sin dominates it always gets in the way of our enjoyment of God. Are you enjoying Him?

Freedom to enjoy each other

"The man and woman were naked and felt no shame." (Genesis 2:25) As they both lived in the freedom of truth, so they experienced the freedom to enjoy each other without agenda, selfishness or impurity. Their relationship was not one of give and take, but one of give only. This was not a marriage of convenience or of duty, this was a marriage where they were enjoying one another. When we live in the power of revealed truth it gives to us the freedom to enjoy our relationships, not merely endure them. With truth renewed minds, we can look at those close to us in different ways, experiencing something of freedom that our first parents enjoyed.

Note what happened when sin entered? When God confronts Adam and Eve, Adam says it all with these damning words, "The woman you put here with me…" (Genesis 3:12) All they had together was forgotten, it was her fault so she should take the wrap. Sin does that. It divides us and ensnares the freedom we had so blissfully enjoyed. Are you enjoying each other?

Freedom to enjoy their work

The punishment Adam suffered gives us insight into what he must have enjoyed before sin. "… through painful toil you will eat of it…" (Genesis 3:17) Adam and Eve up to this point had never experienced any pain in relation to the work which God had asked of them. They had named the animals and were working the garden without a hint of distress, discomfort or pain. Work was a pain free zone.

When we learn to walk in the power of truth, when our lives move on the journey of *truthformation*, this can transform the way we address our work, whether it be secular or spiritual – we learn to enjoy it. For many, work is a pain, a place where they feel trapped and unproductive. Truth can change the way we view what we do or even help us to change what we do. You don't have to be a slave to the rat race, through the freedom of truth you can enjoy what you do. Are you enjoying it?

Freedom to enjoy their environment

What a world they lived in, what a garden they worked in. Everything they saw (except one thing) was theirs to rule, partake of and enjoy. God had given it all to them, not just to work, to rule and be the masters of, but to enjoy. Adam and Eve were free to partake of anything and everything within creation. They were called to be at one with the environment around them and learn to live in glorious balance.

When truth renews our minds, this can transform the way we see our world, our city, town and our street. *Truthformation* should make us great citizens of our nation and our locality. Too often the followers of Jesus are reduced to the role of dissenter, instead of getting into the midst of life and investing. Schools need parent governors, towns need councillors and neighbourhoods need contributors. Adam wasn't just passing through, pruning a few plants with a view to moving on, he was there to contribute and improve his environment while enjoying it on the way. Are you enjoying your world?

For some the thought that Jesus came to give us freedom to enjoy is anathema. 'We are not here to enjoy... the world is dying and this is serious stuff.' Believe me, no one knows this better than me, but I've discovered I'm a better worker, a better worshipper and a much better preacher, when I'm enjoying my world, my life, my relationships and my God. Are you free?

Are you seeing victory over sin in the patterns and practices of your life? Are you relishing all that God has granted you? Are you experiencing the freedom, which allows you to enjoy both the don'ts, and the do's, empowering you to say no and say yes?

Truthformation

My deepest prayer is that you know the truth and the truth makes you free.

I'm off for a bar of chocolate.

The Power of Truth

I once read a story about a traveller who whilst exploring somewhere in Africa, came across two boys playing a game with what looked like marbles. As he got a little closer to watch them, he was struck by the way the marbles were shining in the bright African sunshine. His curiosity took him ever nearer to the boys until to his amazement he discovered that they weren't playing with marbles at all; they were in fact playing with diamonds. (Hold everything, let me just go and check my kids den).

Imagine that, playing games with something so precious and valuable. Of course, to the boys these were just stones, but to the traveller, he understood something of their commercial worth in his own country. He could not comprehend how something of such great worth could be treated in such a casual way. The truth was the two little boys did not know what they had.

The journey to truth and the potential *truthformation* which follows can be a little like this. The problem is that many of us have tried to journey in life, all the while thinking those shiny stones were just marbles, when really they were diamonds. The truth is we've struggled on in the same old way because we never realised what precious stones were in the Word and what power they could release to our lives.

David said of God's Words: "They are more precious than gold, than much pure gold…" (Psalm 19:10) That's what this book has been about. I do not pretend or promote what is contained within as the last word on truth, but rather it is an attempt to get us to pick up the precious stones around us and start taking them seriously in our lives. The gems, jewels and gold that are within the Word can revolutionise the quality and purpose of our lives. So as we conclude together, let's remind ourselves why the Truth is so powerful.

The Truth originates with God

The most profound reason why the Word of God is so powerful is because it comes from God Himself. When we read a report or hear a rumour we always want to know where it came from, as this will either add to or detract from the credibility of the word. So it is with God. What He has spoken comes from Him and is a part of Him. Whether it is a word already spoken, hidden in the written Word, the Bible, or it is a word spoken to you directly by God, the truth of where it came from remains an essential element in our understanding its power.

When God spoke to Abraham, in order to affirm the Word to him, He swore an oath. The writer to the Hebrews makes it clear that God could not find another greater than Himself, so He swore the oath "by Himself." God wanted to make His purpose to Abraham and his descendants very clear, so he spoke and confirmed it. The Bible says: "God did this so that, by two unchangeable things in which it is impossible for God to lie, we who have fled to take hold of the hope offered to us may be greatly encouraged." (Hebrews 6:13-20) What two unchangeable things is God referring to?

They are:

His Character and His Word!

Not only are we encouraged by what was said, but by who said it. There is great power in truth because truth comes from God and God, well, He is God! The precious Bible you are holding in your hand, that word which you have hidden in your heart, both have power, because both have come from God. It is important we remind ourselves of this, so that we focus on who said it, as much as on what it says.

The Truth aligns us with the eternal

David said: "The statutes of the Lord are trustworthy, making wise the simple." (Psalm 19:7) The Truth, the Word is the revelation of a higher wisdom contained within the Kingdom of God. That which has been given to us is not just the result of thousands of years of clever people recording their thoughts, rather it is the wisdom of heaven, the code of God's kingdom. It is light and revelation from a higher level altogether.

In teaching us of the wisdom of God, Paul wrote: "No eye has seen, no ear has heard, no mind has conceived what God has prepared for those who love Him."

Now this is where many stop, but it's the next bit which is really exciting: "… but God has revealed it to us by His Spirit." (1 Corinthians 2:10)

Paul further argued that those who have received the Spirit of God can understand the things God has freely given, while the man without the Spirit of God: "… does not accept the things that come from the Spirit of God, for they are foolishness to him, and he cannot understand them, because they are spiritually discerned." (2:14)

The Truth is so powerful because it is not merely an earth-based wisdom, which can be learned by intellectual development. Rather it is a heaven-based wisdom, which comes by revelation through the Spirit of God. So the fact that we may have received and know truth means we are already beginning to look at the world differently and that we can address it with wisdom that is out of the box as far as our planet is concerned. Understood and used properly, this gives us great power.

Too many followers of Jesus take their lead from the tabloids, the chat shows or the silver screen. Although I believe we can learn from everything, the Truth we are speaking of here cannot be learned from any of these places, only from God. Having got it, this empowers us to see and understand the world differently. Why do we shy away from debate, from politics and from engaging with our world? With such truth and wisdom comes great power. Is it any wonder Paul concluded: "So we fix our eyes not on what is seen, but on what is unseen. For what is seen is temporary, but what is unseen is eternal." (2 Corinthians 4:18)

The Truth connects us to the supernatural

If we live by natural truth it produces natural results. If we live by supernatural truth it produces supernatural results. Sometimes God's Truth so flies in the face of all we have been taught, that without revelation it would be difficult to go with it. God says if you want to

Truthformation

live, then you must die. If you want to be free, you must be bound and if you want to get, then you must give! Unfortunately over the years the Church has represented God's Truth in ways that has made everyone involved look foolish, but it would be unwise to throw the baby away with the bath water. The basic fact remains, the revealed Truth of God is supernatural in nature, and if obeyed, will produce supernatural results.

Firstly, it gives us supernatural foundation. The builders of Matthew seven were tested about what they built on. The foolish man who built on what he knew outside of God was found to be wanting, whereas the wise man who built on what God said, saw a different result from that which might have been expected. The storm may have had the power to knock both houses down, but one stood, because one was built on obedience to supernatural truth, which produced supernatural results.

I appreciate the genius of many people outside of Christ and I have learned to listen and respect contributions from those who fundamentally may discard the Bible. However, appreciating is one thing, building my life upon it is another. God's got the jump on wisdom.

Secondly, it provides us with supernatural illumination. David said of the Truth: "Your word is a lamp to my feet and a light to my path." (Psalm 119:105)

Without truth, we are at the mercy of the darkness, for where there is no light, darkness reigns. A number of years ago I visited the Yorkshire Mining Museum. Now that is one job I just could not have done, so its hats off to anyone who went down a dark, damp hole to dig more dark, damp holes. When we descended the few hundred feet in the cage, our guide gave us the drill and led us around the various exhibitions. At one point he stopped the party and asked them to turn their torches off (we all had them attached to our helmets). I will never forget what happened next. The darkness enveloped us instantly and I want to assure you I could not see a thing. I even held my hand right up to my eye and still could not see it. It was the only place I've ever been where there was absolutely no light. Had the guide left us there, we would have been lost forever. Without light, even a little light, we were at the mercy of the darkness.

When we live outside of God's revealed truth, we deprive our mind of light. It's like being down that mineshaft. No light is getting to our thought processes and hence to our behaviour. The longer this continues the more we expose ourselves to the dangers contained within the darkness. The scary thing is though, the more we live in the darkness, the more we get used to it and we become convinced that how we are thinking and living is okay. Everything changes when someone switches the light on.

The light provides illumination for our mind's processes and the life paths we are going to take. It helps us to make the right choices and go the right way. It ensures we are not powerless, groping in the dark, but the light empowers us to see where we are, where we are going and how we are to get there. Reason without the truth and your reasoning is purely natural and it will leave you in the dark. Learn to embrace the truth and the light will come on, showing you the way, and ensuring you will never be at the mercy of the darkness again.

Thirdly, it empowers us to supernatural transformation. This has been the theme of the whole book. God spoken revelation truth renews our minds, enabling us to resist being conformed to the fashion or mould of the planet and empowering us to change completely from the inside out. People can change naturally by natural means. By sheer force of will power they can overcome the most incredible odds. However, if we want to change supernaturally, we need supernatural empowerment and this comes only from the truth.

I can remember as a young person, struggling with issues of guilt and condemnation in my life. Coming from a Protestant tradition we prided ourselves in justification by faith… not works! Yet the reality was I continually engaged in what I called Protestant Penance. When I failed God, I would end up fasting and praying for days on end trying to get assurance that He truly had forgiven me of that sin. Can you imagine what it was like if I committed the same sin while repenting of the first one? Layer upon layer of guilt was upon me, and with it all joy disappeared. Heaven seemed like brass when I prayed and my non-Christian friends seemed to be enjoying life more than I was. But then one day it changed. I was praying in my room and a verse came into my mind, it was 1 John 1:9. I did not know what it said, just where it was. So I looked it up and read these words: "If we confess our sins, He is faithful and just and will forgive us our sins and purify us from all unrighteousness."

A light came on and I saw this truth for the first time. That day a supernatural transformation took place in my bedroom. I got up from

Truthformation

my knees guiltless, free and empowered. This was not down to reason or logic, it all happened because my spirit and my mind connected with the supernatural truth of God's word.

Harry Houdini, the famous escapologist issued a challenge wherever he went. He claimed he could be locked in any jail cell in the country and within a short time he could escape. However, one time something went wrong. After being placed in a jail cell, he took from his belt a concealed piece of metal, strong and flexible. He set to work immediately, but something seemed very unusual about this particular lock. Thirty minutes past, then an hour and the great man was by now bathed in sweat and panting in exasperation, but still he could not pick the lock. Finally after two hours or so he collapsed in frustration and failure falling against the door he could not open, but as he did so, it swung wide. It had not been locked. He was free and he didn't know it. Got the picture? Why die in a prison cell of ignorance, when revelation truth can renew your mind, transform your life and set you free.

There is power in the Truth, but the power is only released as we receive it, hear it and put it into practice. This process releases the power and the result is a life of transformation. I've called this journey *truthformation*, because I have come to understand both by revelation and experience, that truth is the only means by which a man or a woman can change.

My prayer for you is this, that today and for the rest of your life, you will know a revelation of truth, the power to change and the joy of living in freedom. If you know the truth, it will set you free.

John Andrews

Appendix
People of the Word

If we are to be people who continually engage with *truthformation*, then we must be passionate lovers and devotees of the Word. This is not a preoccupation with chapter, verse and text, but a sincere engagement with truth. Throughout my life I have met many people who could quote 'chapter and verse' of the Book and yet who lived in a way that contradicted everything the Book advocates. It is not enough to know what the Bible says, rather we must endeavor to know what it means!

Men and women who walk in transformation are those who relentlessly open their heart and spirit to the truth. They know that it is 'knowing' the truth which forms the principle key to living in the power of real, radical and lasting change.

Here are some tips to getting the Word inside you:

Want It
Desire is the key to so much in our lives. If you don't see the importance of it then you will never set it as a priority. It is amazing what you will do if you want to and if you believe it is vital.

Read It
I am amazed at how many followers of Jesus do not read the Word on a regular basis. I am not going to tell you how to do it, because then you'll do it my way and it will become more a matter of religion than relationship, but I will presume to give you a little guidance.
- *Use a modern version of the Bible*
- *Variety is the spice of life* - Don't just read the bits you like or one area, try dipping into the Old and New Testaments at the same time.
- *Little and often*. It is better to eat regularly than to starve and binge. One

chapter per day with meaning and understanding is a good target. It's also good for your health and you digestive system.

- *Attainable goals*

So many wonderful well intentioned people set targets that are out of reach. If you're a parent and you're holding down three part-time jobs, then 20 chapters of Leviticus a day may be a little over ambitious. Relax, it isn't a competition. Not including a leap year there are 365 days in a year. Just think, one chapter per day and you could read the New Testament almost one and a half times. Wow! You can do it.

Listen to It

If you are struggling to read it, then why not invest in a set of cds and listen to it? I have a version with music and crashing waves, it's great. I know, I know you can't afford cds, even without waves... then get a friend with a great voice to read it onto tape for you. Although make sure they can read well.

If you miss the teaching ministry of your church, buy the CDs... no, just buy the CDs anyway. One of my best friends John, listens to every series on CD we teach at church, even if he was there for the live gig. The amount of times he has shared with me things he's 'heard' second time around proves the worth of listening to the Word and that sermon again.

Memorise It (Write It)

I am told that people young and old just can't memorise things, especially Scripture. I do not accept this at all. For the last sixteen years I have worked off and meditated on the NIV version of the Bible, and yet today I can still quote verses I learned as a child in Good News clubs... from the King James version! Try to learn one statement of truth from the Bible per week for a month or two and see what happens.

But if you really can't memorise it, then why not write it down. Put it in your diary, your computer or under your fridge magnet (I know you've got one). These truth 'snacks' may just help change the way you think and what you think about.

Confess It

Confession really is good for the soul. There is a powerful link to what we believe and what we speak. If God has deposited truth into your life, then it is a powerful and positive practice to consistently confess that truth. The Bible is not only full of confession; much of it is a confession.

Enjoy It

Remember, the Word of God is not a chore. Although it contains many tough and challenging words, it should nonetheless be approached with joy. The Bible isn't like going to the dentist (no offence intended to any dentists), an experience to be survived and endured, this is a glorious book of life and health. 'Getting through it' will probably mean you'll miss it. Enjoy it, it really is good for you!

Listen to David, a lover of truth.
> "They (God's Words) are more precious than gold,
> than much pure gold, they are sweeter than honey,
> than honey from the comb. By them your servant is warned,
> in keeping them there is great reward."
> *Psalm 19:10-11*

**Truth is the key to transformation.
Embrace it and live.**

Other books by John Andrews available from
www.esbresources.co.uk

Rest   £5.99

God has given us REST so that we may enjoy life and in turn be great adverts for His life on the earth. Too many of us are working and not resting, living and not laughing, achieving and not enjoying. Look at Jesus, He had the weight of the world on His shoulders and yet He was a man at REST, loving people, living life joyfully while still totally focused on His mission.

Loved   £6.99

Why is the God who is love, the best kept secret in the universe? You would think that such a prospect would be celebrated and enjoyed in the Church, trumpeted and proclaimed to a dying world. Yet somehow, this glorious truth, this life-giving message, this world-changing power, has been among the most neglected in pulpits and in mission. The story that God is love, languishes in dusty recesses, under a pile of issues deemed weightier and more important. But what could be more important than the understanding that at the heart of the universe, at the core of the Church and in the engine room of mission, lies the unshakeable, immeasurable reality that God is love?

Hope   £5.99

This book is a celebration of Hope and a journey to Hope and in it you will discover a practical step by step guide to living a life of Hope. God wants you to be a person who has a belief system empowered by Hope, expressing itself in hopeful dreams, actions and lifestyles. Hope-filled people impact their world with life and optimism. They defy the odds, destroy cynicism and create a culture where dreams are given every opportunity to come true.

Mission is Like a Box of Chocolates   £7.99

Imagine receiving a never ending supply of chocolate. Every delight and delicacy you can think of, given as a free gift... and all yours! But imagine keeping all that chocolate to yourself, gorging selfishly each day, content with the goal of self-satisfaction, while so many around you have never tasted your special chocolate even once and others don't even know it exists. This book calls those who have already received Heaven's Chocolate to consider sharing it with those who have never tasted it and others who don't know it exists, that our focus would move away from asking for more, to looking at ways in which we can share what we have.

Moving Beyond Mediocrity   £7.99

Moving Beyond Mediocrity is a book written to help us negotiate such a journey. Too many want to arrive at destinations of success cheaply and easily. They want glory without pain, recognition without rejection, prosperity without generosity and as much success with as few shakes as possible. However, as someone once said, 'there are no short-cuts to anywhere that's worth going.' Though God's plans for us are hope-filled and glorious, the journey to them will not be without turbulence. The serious pilgrim seeks to understand this truth and settle it within them once and for all.'

About the author

Dr John Andrews has been in full-time Christian leadership since 1987 and the leader of Rotherham New Life since 1997, during which time the church has undergone significant change. As well as being Senior Leader of Rotherham New Life Christian Centre, he is Director of Training at Mattersey Hall College and Graduate School, taking up this post on 1st September 2006. He also serves on the General Superintendancy team of Asemblies of God UK.

Born in Belfast, Northern Ireland, John is married Dawn and together they have three children, Elaina, Simeon and Beth-Anne. He is a graduate of the Assemblies of God Bible College, Mattersey Hall. He holds a Masters degree in Pentecostal and Charismatic Studies from Sheffield University and a Doctorate from the University of Wales.

He is a teacher with a passion to inspire and equip the Church to make God famous in their world. As well as ministering in the UK, John travels regularly to various nations of the world seeking to invest what he has, while he can.

John's hobbies include supporting his beloved football team Liverpool, listening to music, reading and watch great movies with his favourite movie of all time being It's a Wonderful Life. He loves to eat and among his favourite food groups are, Chinese, Italian and CHOCOLATE!!!